## Dedication(s)

Whenever I read a book, I'm always interested to see who the author has dedicated their work to. In most cases it's a single person such as 'For my mother/father/husband' etc, or perhaps it will be for the person who inspired the writer to put pen to paper.

In my case, I guess if I'm to choose one person, then this really should be dedicated to my husband. I don't tell him nearly enough how much I love him and when he took my hand and led me onto the crazy rollercoaster we both ride through life, I never could have imagined what an incredible journey we would be making together. He drives me mad at times (isn't that in the job description for 'Husband') but we're a great team and I hope I make him proud.

When I think of the *inspiration* for this book, then that has to be my dog Diesel. He was the one who caused me to begin to look at my pets and all other canines in such a different way, but since then I've learnt so much from each of the dogs in my life, it would be impossible to list them all. They, and I, know who they are and that will suffice, I hope.

Finally, as well as the above, I think I'd also like to dedicate this book to YOU. This is as a thank you for taking the time to read it, and for hopefully telling your friends about it too so that they can also receive their own dedication.

Thank you. I hope you enjoy sharing my experiences.

# Table of Contents

**Bringing Home a New Born Baby into the House**


**The Last Word**

# Introduction

*"I promise you, Margaret, if ever I get around to writing my book, then you'll <u>definitely</u> be in it!!"*

*So here goes….*

The call had come in from a particularly well spoken gentleman who told me all about his unruly German Shepherd Dog. Around 10 months old and characteristically strong, the GSD had become a bit of a nightmare on walks as he was behaving unpredictably around other dogs. Having asked the gentleman if he had any friends or neighbours with dogs who we could perhaps arrange to meet 'accidentally on purpose' on a walk, we had planned to meet up with Margaret. My client and his wife knew this lady as the manager of their local Post Office and she was also the owner of two, rather elderly and world weary dogs.

So it came to be that our little troupe of three dog owners, three dogs and one chilly canine psychologist were trudging around an extremely muddy field on a cold and windy November evening. We'd decided to use a local farmer's field to introduce the dogs – with permission of course - and had taken the GSD to meet up with the two older cross-breeds. (Okay, I'm being politically correct there – they were 100% 'Heinz 57 varieties' mongrels – *probably the best dogs you can get in a 'been there, done that, got the t-shirt kind of way, and perfect for helping with doggy socialization.)*

After taking note of the body language the GSD was displaying, I felt fairly confident that his 'problem' wasn't that he was being aggressive, but that he was actually desperate to play. After careful consideration and plenty of discussion around what we would do if 'Plan A' didn't work, it was time to release each of the dogs in turn.

Firstly we released the younger of Margaret's dogs and he just sniffed the ground and had a little wander. The GSD remained fairly relaxed so we unleashed the second, older, dog. This poor little fella was so elderly and decrepit that he literally just stood still, staring in to space, completely oblivious to us and his surroundings.

*Then it was time to take a deep breath… and release the Shepherd.*

He was so excited at being off-leash for the first time in weeks that he completely ignored both of the other dogs and bounded round in a huge circle, circumnavigating us all with a continual 'whoop' of delight. After around five minutes of this he decided that he wanted to get us involved too, so from a distance of around 100 meters, he began to aim straight for us with his ears flapping in the wind and his huge paws covering considerable ground at a breakneck speed!

Luckily, the couple who owned the GSD managed to jump nimbly out of his way, perhaps having seen this type of behavior before. Unfortunately for poor Margaret though, she wasn't quite so fast, and in no time at all the GSD was upon us. He ran, head-first, into Margaret's legs, taking her swiftly off her feet and depositing her with a heavy thump, face down in the mud and with her back-side in the air.

*At this point, the eldest of her dogs, and the one who had appeared to only just have the energy to breathe, let alone get involved in any physical activity, took it on himself to jump excitedly onto Margaret's protruding back-side, clinging on and humping for all he was worth.*

*That funny little dog with the grey crinkly hair and the spindly, arthritic legs seemed to be saying, "Finally woman, after all these years, I've at last got you right where I want you!!!"*

And this, dear reader, is just a glimpse of the weird and wacky life of a canine psychologist. You name it and I've probably seen it. If your dog's done it, mine probably did it too and it was thanks to this very need to sort out my own 'doggy problems' that my life took a course that I had never imagined in my wildest dreams….

**In the Beginning….**

Some people believe in fate. The belief that, somehow, the whole of our lives are predetermined and mapped out, in advance, right down to the very last detail. As though some celestial being - perhaps even God Himself - has booked every date in your diary up to, and including, the very moment when your life is over.

Your 'number is up' and that's your time to go. Just as it always would have been, *because, like it or not,* **your** *bus stops here.* No matter what you do to your body throughout your lifetime, whether you smoke, drink, eat junk food, or jump out of aeroplanes wearing nothing more for safety than a flimsy piece of silk, tied together with a few strategically placed wires, *if your number comes out of the big lottery machine in the sky, your time has come and you'd better just accept it!*

Some say that fate decides for us who will be the love of our lives. When and where we will meet that person, no matter how unlikely it may seem that our paths should ever cross. If it's 'written in the stars' then it's a certainty, regardless of how strange or coincidental that particular meeting may be. Fate plans our families, our careers, our health, wealth and happiness and it can't be changed because it's just the way it's meant to be.

Then again, some people believe that we make and shape our own destiny. That if 'we *think* it then we can *be* it'. Followers of 'cosmic ordering' or 'The Secret' (check out www.thesecret.tv) believe that we can choose whatever we want in life, however unobtainable it may at first appear to be. By simply asking, we will receive. Even the bible tells us this and so perhaps it's not such a bizarre concept after all? Millions of people follow the bible and believe its teachings so there may be some truth in that particular idea, however strange it might seem.

If we want something bad enough, and we focus on that one specific goal hard enough, the Universe will move heaven and earth to guarantee that we receive it. We're told that when following 'The Secret' we shouldn't worry about *how* the thing we want will manifest itself, but we should just concentrate on the end result. The Universe will sort out the intricacies for us, so if we want the big house and the flash car we shouldn't concern ourselves with the fact that we only earn enough to support a one bedroom flat and a Ford Fiesta as if we 'visualise' ourselves in the house and driving the car, the Universe will find a way to make it real.

Alternatively, there are those who believe in nothing at all. We, as the human race, just *are*. Nothing guides us, nothing provides for us (except ourselves) and nothing plans out our lives. We simply go through life's journey facing numerous decisions and crossroads and we have to work it out for ourselves, perhaps with the support and advice of our loved ones. Whichever road we take, we will just end up at the other end, wherever that may be. Although we may hit life's potholes along the way, some worse than others, whatever happens we'll find a way to deal with it and life will just go on.

*All very confusing - and, I appreciate, nothing to do with dogs!!*

Yet, despite having my own thoughts on each of the above, when I look back on what happened to me in the late 1990's, it certainly feels as though fate had a very strong hand in my life at that particular time. The events which would unfold over a period of around three years were never planned by me and were not the subject of my dreams or aspirations.

I was about to be sent on a journey, which would not only be full of surprises and special moments, but which I would not have believed possible had I been shown it in a crystal ball. Moments which would provide me, and many others, with plenty of laughs, tears and feelings of such overwhelming satisfaction, that I had never imagined could be possible.

Fate, the Universe, or simply circumstance, brought about a particular chain of events that would result in me becoming a qualified and highly experienced Canine Psychologist, with an insight into the minds of our four legged, doggy friends that I'd never have anticipated in a million years. It has brought me into contact with hundreds of owners who were at their wit's end with the behaviour of their poochie pals and who, in the majority of cases, have seen me as some kind of 'dog charmer' with magical powers and the ability to change their lives in the same way that mine was changed over twelve years ago.

On many occasions I've been told, by clients, friends and relatives, that I should write a book. I won't try to deny that it's not something I've thought about since being very young, but I'd never really had any subject matter before. I'd tried my hand at fiction, but found that:

My stories weren't very interesting

I ran out of things to say

I'd said everything I wanted to within the first two pages

In recent years, however, the subject matter has pretty much written itself. I've had so many great and heart-warming experiences that I feel compelled to share just a few of them with you and I hope you will then pass them onto your loved ones too so that they can join in the fun. I've seen all manner of memorable things since dogs took over my life and I'm now delighted to give you, the reader, just a small glimpse of my crazy world.

From extremely scary incidents involving vacuum cleaners to seriously randy OAP pooches (see earlier), I'd like to think I've seen it all, but whenever I start to believe that, something else will come along to surprise and delight me. No two cases can ever be truly the same, although I have tended to see patterns form. It's wrong to tar all dogs of any particular type with the same brush, but there are very obvious similarities in the problems I see in some breeds.

Dogs are now a major part of my life, both as my own pets, for I have many of my own, and as a result of my canine behaviour consultancy - Doggy Dilemmas. That said, every day I learn something new about the way in which these wonderful animals live their lives. The way they communicate with me, with each other and what makes them 'tick'.

Despite this ever increasing knowledge, I still feel that I've only just scratched the surface of what goes on inside their heads. They have such individual personalities it's like watching children develop. From tiny puppies to elderly 'plodders' they demonstrate a huge array of emotions from love and affection to jealousy and even hatred.

Much the same as people, they can occasionally meet someone (or some dog) that they simply don't like. I can easily relate to this point and I'm sure that you can too. It's always amazed me how we can meet someone totally new and immediately hit it off and find them fascinating, almost like a 'soul mate'. On another occasion we can perhaps meet someone else and feel an immediate dislike and prickliness towards that person with absolutely no foundation for those feelings whatsoever.

Over the rest of these pages I'm going to relate a number of stories which I hope you will enjoy. They are all true and many still make me smile, or cry, as the case may be. For the purpose of saving anyone any embarrassment, I haven't revealed the true names of my clients and have instead given them false identities. I hope if any of them are reading this book, they will forgive me for including their particular tales and will be proud of the fact that they were memorable enough to be included, considering that I've seen hundreds of 'doggy dilemmas' over the years.

I also hope that you, the reader, may learn something from my writing. I purposely didn't want this book to be just another dog-training manual, as I believed that a volume of that type would only appeal to those who currently own a dog and I'd like to think this is more than that. Towards the end of my story, however, I will give advice that I feel could be helpful or appropriate.

At times, when an incident occurs, or a particular course of action is taken which I feel should have been handled in a different way, I may offer my opinion as to how I feel things could have been improved. I stress at this point, that it is only MY opinion. The problem with dog training is that EVERYONE is an expert. However, I do feel I'm pretty well qualified to call myself such by now, although even I, with a wealth of experience, can potentially encounter something totally new with each dog I meet.

In addition, towards the end of the book, I include a section on how to deal with or prevent a range of problems from soiling, chewing, barking and more.

For anyone requiring further assistance with their own canine behaviour problems I would highly recommend seeking the help of a reputable consultant in your own area. Please try to avoid anyone who uses outdated methods which seem to bully a dog into submission.

Yes, it can be important to be seen as the master, but to do this using the type of body language and signals that a dog will understand, rather than a choke chain, a heavy hand and an element of fear, will create a far more harmonious partnership with a dog. If in doubt ask your vet to recommend someone, or go on word of mouth by asking around other dog owners you may know.

Once again, I'd like to thank you for taking this leap of faith and purchasing my book. It's always a gamble as to what one may find and, as the saying goes, 'you can't judge a book by its cover' so I'm grateful for your urge to find out what's happening inside. Hopefully I won't disappoint, as choosing which particular stories to tell hasn't been easy and I'm sorry about those that have been excluded. Perhaps if all goes well, there will be more to come....

## Animals, Animals, Animals

For as long as I can remember I've had an incredible love of animals. My Mam tells me that when I was a baby she had a dog called Candy which used to sit by my pram for hours on end, keeping guard so to speak. I never had any true recollection of Candy and had actually imagined her to be white, and a little like a Westie, but when I finally did see an old cine film of her, I was surprised to find that she was a very dark curly haired dog, closely resembling a toy poodle.

I also recall from my childhood that we had a white budgie called Bobby. I loved him as much as any young child can ever truly love a budgie as, despite being a very attractive pet, there's not an awful lot that can be done with them in terms of play etc. However, when we moved house to a nicer part of town, Bobbie was re-homed, or so I believe, as his constant seed spillage wouldn't quite suit our lovely new carpet!

I had a guinea-pig called Squeaker who, again, I don't remember very well at all, except for the fact that, yes, he undoubtedly lived up to his name and we used to hear him calling from his hutch at all hours of the morning. I was a typical child who chose to pester her parents for a pet and then proceeded to take no notice of it whatsoever once the initial appetite was satiated.

As I write this, it is my youngest nephew's birthday and when I visited this evening I was introduced to his 'present' which was two guinea-pigs together in a hutch. I must admit that I asked him if he's helping to clean them out etc and he said he was but a little voice inside was telling me that, seeing this scenario as an adult, I can imagine that it will be no time at all before my sister-in-law is, instead, the guardian of the guineas.

My longest lasting and favourite non-canine pet from my childhood was my rabbit Toshka. He was a gorgeous animal who looked exactly like the wild rabbits we see each day in the countryside. He came from my next-door neighbour's grandfather who had taken him on but, I assume, had found him too much to cope with due to his advancing years.

My neighbours had a huge white, female rabbit called Flash who sadly ended up, we believe, in the pot of a passing tinker (commonly thought of as a gypsy, but being of Romany origin myself, I refuse to sully the name of my ancestors' kind by calling him that). He had entered my neighbours' garden to ask if the family had 'any old iron' as the saying goes and had commented on the rabbit's size and that she looked good enough to eat.

Sure enough, the next morning she was gone and it was obvious, even to a child, that she hadn't let herself out of the hutch. This act was surely the most heinous of crimes and I can only imagine the devastation my neighbouring friends must have felt when they considered the fate of their furry little pal. I truly hope that she gave that tinker the worst bout of diarrhoea and sickness of his life.

One afternoon my own rabbit, Toshka, (or Tosh as he was more commonly called) was in the garage running around where I used to allow him to play freely in an attempt to keep his nails short. I noticed something on his underbelly which alarmed me a little so I called my Dad over to come and examine the problem. After careful consideration, my Dad sat me down and said that it looked very much as though Tosh had a nasty growth on his stomach and that it would need to be seen by a vet. In addition, he gently explained to me that it was possible that the vet would say that there was nothing he could do for Tosh and he may have to be put to sleep. This thought horrified me and I held my bunny closely as I contemplated taking him to the vets.

And so it was that my best friend and I, aged I guess, around 11 years old, headed to the vets with poor Tosh in tow. It was the summer 1976 - the hottest on record for many, many years, and perhaps it even still is. There was a major drought and people even had to turn to stand-pipes in the streets for water. Hose-pipes were strictly prohibited and because this was in the days before we knew better, we all had the best sun-tans ever.

My Dad had to go to work and my Mam had neither a car, nor a driving licence, so the only affordable way to get the vets was on the bus. This, though, was no ordinary bus ride as the journey required a change at the central station and a second bus to the vets from the town centre. All the while, poor Tosh was sweating away in a huge shopping bag! The bag did have a solid square base, but he was very hot inside the make-shift carry case and looking back I'm surprised he didn't die of heat stroke before even reaching the vets.

Eventually we arrived at our destination and explained to the receptionist that we feared my lovely pet rabbit had a growth. She directed us to a treatment room and inside was a stern looking vet and his kindly nurse. Peering into the shopping bag the vet asked me what the problem was so I explained that I had noticed this thing on his stomach and my Dad had suggested that it may be a growth. Mustering all the courage I could find, whilst shuffling on the spot to take my mind off what was coming from between my quivering lips, which I now bit down on harshly to hold back any tears, I went on to say that I understood it might be serious and my Dad had said that if it was cancerous I was to let the vet put my beloved friend to sleep.

The vet and his nurse took the shopping bag from me and as the lady held the bag open, the vet gently pulled Tosh from what, looking back, must have felt by that point like a mobile sauna. He placed my darling pet on the surgery table and asked me to show him the growth. I gently prodded at Tosh's fur and peered at his underbelly until I spotted the nasty, horrible thing that may threaten to take him away from me.

*The conversation went thus - and I can recall every single, excruciating second of it....*

*"There" I said. "That's it."*

*"Where?" asked the vet.*

*"There, look, right there, that skin coloured lump..." I replied*

*"He's a boy" said the vet.*

*"Yes, I KNOW he's a boy!" I said, feeling increasingly anxious.*

And, of course, the vet replied…..*"But that's WHY he's a boy!!!!!!"*

Cue the hasty departure of two VERY embarrassed young ladies, leaving behind a highly amused vet and a nurse who was almost on the floor with laughter!!

After relaying the story to my Mam, interspersed with fits of the giggles, she told me that she would speak to my Dad when he got in from work, but that I should be around to listen in.

As he walked through the door, their conversation went as follows...

*"Did our Jo take Tosh to the vets?"*

*"Yes, she did, poor little fella.  Two bus trips in all that heat"*

*"So, is it a growth then?"*

 *"Yep, sure is."*

*"And, is the vet going to take it off then?"*

*"Yep, he is……*

*Oh, and....by the way....he's booked you in to remove YOURS next week!!!"*


Tosh lived to the ripe old age of ten, and died just a few weeks before I was due to leave home and had been debating whether or not it would be fair to take him with me.  It felt almost as though he'd made the decision for me and he was still slightly warm when I arrived home from work to find him lying peacefully in his hutch, in the gentle summer breeze.

Despite having had that particularly scary experience in his younger days, he has left me with this wonderful tale.  It's the kind, I believe, one likes to tell after a few too many beers when chatting amongst friends and loved ones.  *And my poor Dad will NEVER live it down!*

## My First 'Best Friend'

The first dog I ever had as my very own was Scrapper and at the time I took him on I was living with my then boyfriend, (now an ex) whose old school chum had owned the bitch whose pup he was. We moved in together and I suddenly felt, rightly or wrongly, that I was now mature and responsible enough to own a dog. A dog that would be mine, and mine only, rather than a family pet.

Scrapper was a scraggy terrier cross of indeterminate heritage who would become my best pal from the minute I left home and who had come into my life as a tiny, six week old, puppy (an age which is considered way too young to separate a pup from the litter nowadays, but things were much different back then). His mother was a large Yorkshire terrier type dog but the father was unknown. 'Scraps' was the product of a clandestine liaison between a runaway bitch and, in all probability, the local 'jack the lad' of the canine world, and whose identity remains a mystery to this day.

When I think of that lovely little scruff, I now know that I did everything wrong that an owner possibly can, and therein lay the problem. This would continue with every dog I owned up until the point that an enormous light-bulb came on above my head, but that is for the future. In the meantime, Scrapper was my little darling, who will remain forever special in my heart and whose end was not only one of my life's saddest moments, but one that would fill me with uncertainty about how much say we should have in how our animals meet their end, but again, that's for later.

In the meantime, he had a very happy life which was mostly without incident. However, there are a couple of situations that I always recall with fondness when I think of Scrapper and my time with him before I met my husband...

Whilst sitting outside in the sun one morning, my ex and I heard the usual rumpus as the postman arrived. Scrapper ran to the hallway and hurled himself at the door with his familiar gusto - one which the continually changing paper boys would have to learn to deal with. *We never saw the same kid for long and I used to wonder if Scraps had anything to do with that.*

I went to retrieve the mail and found the dog with a post-card in his mouth from a friend who was on holiday in America. Across the card was a large, bubbly smear of blood! *"Oh no!"* I exclaimed, *"I wonder if he's bitten the postie?"* Thoughts of litigation and whether or not a 'Beware of the Dog' sign would keep me out of court began to wash through my mind. Vivid images of leaving the house, only to find the postie lying in a sea of blood on the doorstep, surrounded by a crowd of angry neighbours tut-tutting as I'd held up their mail delivery, were growing ever more likely in my head.

My ex studied the card for a minute and then uttered,

*"Oh no, look at the blood. Ah, there's a **NAIL**!!!"*

Well, having always been particularly squeamish about nails since a horrible accident in a swimming pool resulted in me unwittingly ripping one from my toe as a child, I almost passed out at the thought. I recoiled in horror as my panicked eyes checked out the offending card, trying to half see said nail, and half avoid seeing it.

*"Where?!"* I yelled, feeling increasingly apprehensive at the thought of seeing the end of the postie's finger stuck to the back of the item he'd delivered with such care, before losing a pint of blood thanks to a savaging by the local manic mongrel....

*"On the door, of course"* said the ex, *"Scrapper's cut his nose on the nail that's sticking out by the letterbox!!!"*

Needless to say, that was one time when I was happy to see my dog's nose bleeding, rather than something else! The nail was hammered in, a 'Beware of the Dog' sign took pride of place on the door, and Scrapper was confined to the lounge whenever the postie was due - just in case.

*Although it can be possible to train your dog to stop lunging at the mail, if I'm honest, the best way to prevent this type of thing is to install a post basket or, even better, a box on the wall on the outside of the property.. He may stop doing it whilst you're around, but even if you train it out of him, there's a chance he'll still 'have a go' when alone, so for the safety of both dog and postie, I'd recommend this course of action.*

Another incident that happened with Scrapper involved a local butcher. We were walking back from the park when I popped into the shop to get some meat for the evening meal and the butcher spied Scrapper waiting patiently outside. Insisting that his home made dog meal (a type of mince and offal product which I suppose was created in an attempt to use up every last bit of the meat, whilst making him a profit in the process) was, he said, the very best in the area and he tried to convince me to buy some for Scrapper.

I told him that I was happy enough with the dog food I used and wouldn't bother, thank you. *(Although this statement was to become an eye-opener for me in the future as I would learn about animal nutrition and also that I had been feeding poor Scrapper pretty badly in the early days).*

Plus, I protested, that I couldn't always be sure I could get to the shop due to work commitments so I didn't want to change the dog's diet to something I couldn't guarantee to continue with. However, he was reluctant to accept my excuse and he encouraged me to follow him as we ventured out into the street - the butcher carrying a handful of some dodgy looking meat based product, and me displaying a barely concealed look of bemusement.

Despite the butcher shoving repeated handfuls of 'meal' under his nose, Scrapper wasn't interested at all. In fact, I'd never actually known him turn his nose up at anything, so it can't have been too good. Undeterred by this behaviour, the butcher carried on in his relentless attempts at proving just how great his produce was.

Finally, in desperation and full view of the whole of the passing public, in fact right beside a busy bus route and thoroughfare, the butcher proceeded to kneel down on the grubby pavement beside Scrapper, whilst proclaiming for all to see, *"Yum yum, doggy, this is lovely!"* and *"This is the best dog meal in town"* and pretending to eat the mush.

After one last sniff, Scrapper turned on his tail, cocked his leg beside the butcher in the ultimate rebuff of his home made dog meal and gave me a knowing look that almost said, *"Hey Mam, what a pillock eh?"*

In reality, looking back, Scrapper was a 'guinea pig' rather than a dog. We'd had a dog at home with my family - Sandy, a gorgeous rough collie - but her training etc had all been left to my parents who, in my opinion, did a grand job. I, on the other hand, learnt nothing, which meant that my dog was to become a neurotic, clingy, yapping unsociable house-soiler who would eat his way through a mountain of shoes leaving me in a position where I once had to go to work in my slippers!

## New Life, New Furry Friends

Time moved on and following my split with that particular partner I eventually met and married my now husband, whom I affectionately named Scrum (due to the fact that he was built like a rugby player and pretty 'scrumptious' too).

Second in our doggy dynasty along with Scrapper, came Jessie, or Jessica Pudding as she became affectionately called. Jessie had entered our lives via a little, half empty pet shop in one of the less affluent parts of Hull, but an area in which the inhabitants are considered to be the 'salt of the earth'.

Scrum and I were living in a large, one bedroom, ground-floor flat with a substantial garden at the time we bought Jessie. We were out shopping one afternoon and happened upon the pet shop where we decided to have a look at the fish as we had recently acquired a tropical tank and were keen to add to its population.

Whilst mooching around in the shop, Scrum pointed out a small cage which held this tiny black puppy with a white blaze on its chest, white markings on its paws which made it look as though it was wearing 'stirrup pants' *(if you're under 30, ask your mother)* and a tiny white line under the mouth which looked like a smile.

Out of curiosity, I asked the owner of the shop what sex this puppy was, semi-aware of the fact that I was hatching a plan. When the pup proved to be female - despite constant referrals to it by the shopkeeper as 'he' - then my mind began working overtime.

Later that afternoon, when we returned home, Scrum and I were chatting about the day in general and I happened to ask if he thought the puppy would be taken home by the shopkeeper, rather than spend the night in the cage. I was concerned, as this was Saturday afternoon, and it was unlikely that the shop would open on a Sunday. I shouldn't have doubted that the pup would not be cared for properly, but after all, we were talking about a fairly dodgy part of town, so who could be certain?

Making a pretty lame excuse that I was going out to collect some milk (bearing in mind that we'd been to the supermarket earlier in the day), I got on my bicycle and peddled like fury down to the pet shop as the time was nearing 5pm and I expected they might close. Money was a problem that, for once, I wasn't going to let stand in my way. Although I had nothing left in my purse, I DID have my cheque book and handed over the payment of just £10, which was all I needed to take home the little bundle of mischief.

Leaving my bike locked up outside of the shop, whilst wondering if it would still bear its wheels by the morning, I carried the tiny, squirming cutie home to our flat and proudly announced that this was Scrapper's new 'baby sister'.

In my unbelievable naivety I thought that the dogs would just get on with one another and that Scrapper would be glad of the canine company. What actually happened was that Jessie took over the majority of our time and poor Scraps was pushed out of the limelight somewhat, which I believe initially drove him to see Jess as a bit of a nuisance.

It probably took a good six months for them to really form a solid friendship, but eventually it came good and they remained firm pals for many years to come. *(Sadly, both are no longer with us but I like to think that they are reunited in a better place where the postman delivers every hour, chocolate buttons grow on trees and there are countless slippers to be chewed).*

In February 1998 I was working full time as a marketing assistant for a small but excellent company called The Health Scheme. This was a 'not for profit' organisation which provided cash benefits towards everyday health expenses such as spectacles, dental treatment and physiotherapy etc. There are many such schemes around the country and this was the one which was local to Hull, my home town.

I loved my job and relished working hard at a combination of sales/marketing and secretarial duties, having only fairly recently been promoted to this particular position. I also thoroughly enjoyed spending time with my colleagues, some of whom I had worked with for a number of years and with whom I felt I had grown and developed as a human being.

Dogs were something that interested me, and I had an understandable affection for my own, but they certainly didn't dominate my thoughts for any particular length of time, and the idea of working with them didn't even enter my head.

Around this time we took on the third in our ever increasing menagerie - Barney, (or 'Barney Button', 'Barnaby Rudge' and latterly 'Uncle Barney'). He was a gorgeous Kennel Club registered Staffordshire Bull Terrier, and my first introduction into the 'bully' world. In his younger days, my husband had been a breeder of 'staffies' and, although some time earlier he had given up this practice, he had. in fact, owned a young puppy when we met.

However, being totally ignorant to the joys of bull breed dogs at that point, and having been 'educated' by an unbelievably biased media, I had thought that all bull-breed dogs were the spawn of the devil. They were regularly demonised in the press for reportedly carrying out savage attacks on all that they encountered and, sadly, I had taken all this as read, without question.

When my hubby then announced that he intended getting another staffie, I refused to accept it and said that there was no way I would be willing to have a dog like that in my house and putting my best mate Scrapper at risk. I complained that staffies weren't pretty dogs - soon to be proved wrong - and that they couldn't possibly be nice if what the papers said was true - *and it MUST be true, BECAUSE it was in the paper!! (Ugh, the naivety of it all.)*

Whether he knew exactly what he was doing, or whether it was pure chance, Scrum then announced that if I wouldn't have a staffie, he would get an English Bull Terrier. Now, I don't want to offend anyone, and least of all the adoring fans of 'bullies', but to the naive mongrel dog owner, this was like a red rag to a bull(dog). He couldn't have picked a more unconventional looking animal and to even contemplate owning something that looked like a sheep with no fur, was inconceivable to little old me. As I say, whether he had anticipated the reaction, I'll never truly know, despite what he may tell me, but it certainly had the desired effect as I immediately relented and agreed that we would choose a *staffie* puppy from the next appropriate litter we saw!

Over the next few weeks we scanned the local paper for advertisements for staffies. Eventually a litter was spotted that my hubby liked the sound of, so off we went to view our potential new puppy pal. I can't quite recall the number in the litter but there was a cute black and white male that we both took a fancy to. Even better, when checking out the pedigree, we spotted that some of the dogs in the pup's heritage were actually those who had been previously owned or bred by Scrum in his staffie breeding days. It seemed that the hand of fate was involved and we agreed to return the next day to collect our 'baby'.

Upon returning to collect the pup, for some reason Scrum had a change of heart and instead chose a brindle male with a white chest and white paws. I wasn't concerned either way as I knew that this was one choice I shouldn't have a hand in as this was going to be HIS dog and he was the expert on the breed. That said, I'll now admit to feeling a little sad that the brindle one wouldn't match our present colour scheme of purely black and white pooches. *(I can't believe I just said that.)*

We took home this little bundle of lumbering love and began to ponder upon a name. Prior to collecting him we had each compiled huge lists of suggested names that we thought would be suitable, but however many times we studied the lists, none of them seemed to fit the bill. Suddenly, without any prompting, we looked at the pup, then looked at one another and declared, *"Barney!"* I don't know why, as that particular name didn't appear on either of our lists, but he just *looked* like a Barney and that's what he became.

Due to work commitments on my part we hadn't been able to collect Barney from the breeder until early in the evening so it wasn't too long before it was time to retire for the night. We gave him some food, a toy and a snuggly blanket. We spread ample layers of newspaper around the small kitchen floor before kissing him goodnight and toddling off to bed.

We hadn't dared leave him with the other two dogs for fear that there could be an accidental injury in the night. Scrapper had seemed fairly indifferent to the whole 'new buddy' affair, but Jessie had been beside herself with joy. Like some ageing spinster, it was almost as though she was listening to her ever hastening body clock and craving a child of her own. Barney was to become that child, and the welcome he had received from her was incredible.

She had put on a tremendous display of affection with continual 'play bows' and snuffling of the puppy to show her affection. However, there was always the possibility that a little overly zealous play could result in one tiny puppy with a broken leg, or even worse, so he was left alone in the kitchen - his first time away from his mother and siblings - *and boy did he protest!*

Within, perhaps, ten minutes of getting into bed there came a noise like nothing I had ever encountered before in my life. Seeming to come from the very soul of this tiny little bundle of loveliness was a sound so disturbing that I half expected a whole force of policemen to come crashing through the front door, in order to save some poor victim from a horrendous torture, involving red hot pokers, the pulling of teeth and lemon juice on numerous paper cuts. The noise was like a combination of a growl, a scream, a bark and a cough, all entwined to form one tremendous cacophony of distress.

Scrum told me at the time that it's a sound like no other and one which he suggested could be quite unique to staffies. He and his friend had previously named the noise 'ockling' (pronounced ockerling) but I doubt that this appears in the dictionary and if it does I don't know how it could truly be put into words! Barney seemed to be crying "Nhoooo, nhoooo" as though refusing to believe that he had been left so alone in this dark and strange environment and feeling certain that, if he protested loud and hard enough, he would be saved. *And do you know what - he was damned well RIGHT!*

No sooner had we got into bed than we were up again, debating what to do about the newly acquired monster in the kitchen. We didn't want to set a precedent by bringing him upstairs, but we both silently knew that neither of us would be willing to shift ourselves to the kitchen, with the prospect of a night on the floor, potentially surrounded by puppy poo. In the end we decided to place him in a large box, with a soft, warm pillow at the bottom. We then brought him upstairs, beside our own bed and thankfully - mainly due to the fact that Scrum slept with his hand inside the box throughout - the little fella slept soundly for the rest of the night....

*From then on, he would never sleep downstairs again and, in time, would progress from the floor to the bed and eventually even to underneath the covers. (I know, my mother would be horrified!) For many wonderful years to come, even in the midst of sleep, we would feel him move and simultaneously lift the duvet to allow him to climb in between us for his nightly snuggle.*

Although I may now occasionally recommend to owners that removing their dog from the bedroom could help to adjust the 'pack' structure, I can't deny that sleeping with your dog is one of the greatest pleasures of canine companionship. One which, since the inevitable loss of Barney, has never quite been matched by any other dog in our lives.

## A Bird in the Hand…

As well as our ever increasing 'pack' of dogs within the house, over the years my husband and I have had several pets of the non canine kind. A number of hamsters have graced our lives although they sadly never seemed to live for too long. We actually bought a couple of sisters from the same litter once but they fought ferociously so had to be housed in cages side by side instead. What was incredibly strange about this pair was that they even DIED on the same day! I checked for a gas leak or contamination of their food and there were no clues to suggest anything other than natural causes but it was very odd indeed.

Having a particular love for all tiny mammals I once bought a gorgeous little brown mouse on a whim whilst shopping - not realising that Scrum wasn't keen on mice at all due to their skinny furless tails. I thought he was wonderful and I named him Boris, giving him pride of place in the kitchen so I could talk to him and give him titbits whilst cooking.

After a week or so Scrum pointed out how I needed to reduce the amount of titbits I was giving Boris as he was getting a little on the rotund side and I had to agree that perhaps I'd overdone it a bit, so I vowed to cut it out. As a result he slimmed down to almost his former size and I wished I'd had the ability to make myself lose weight so easily.

However, a couple of days after noticing just how well his weight-loss programme had gone, I found myself standing in the kitchen listening to an almost inaudible squeak. On closer inspection, I found that the sound was coming from Boris' little mouse-house within the cage and, after berating myself for even beginning to think that perhaps sawdust 'squeaks' when wet, I removed the lid of the house to discover 14 tiny baby mice. *It seemed that Boris was, in fact, an unmarried mother in the shape of Bertha.*

Once they were old enough, and after I had managed to separate the sexes (mice can breed from a very early age and I didn't want an epidemic on my hands), I prepared myself for the distressing task of taking them back to the pet-shop that I had bought Boris/Bertha from, as the owner had agreed to take them on. At the last minute I broke down in tears and admitted that I'd grown really attached to them and couldn't face it, so, after much discussion with Scrum, he reluctantly agreed that I could keep the mice.

Keeping the females together wasn't a problem as they all got along famously, but the males were another story and they fought like crazy. Seeing no other option than to separate them from one another I had to buy six smaller tanks and keep them all on shelves in our spare bedroom. Cleaning and feeding was becoming quite a chore and the noise throughout the night of seven mouse-wheels whirring as their nocturnal playtime began was a bit of a pain to say the least.

One morning the next door neighbour came knocking and asked the question, did we still have all of our mice? As I ran upstairs to check, she told Scrum how she had woken up that morning to find a small brown mouse running through her shoulder length hair!!! Thankfully all of my little furry friends were still safe in their homes, and I was certain that it was totally ridiculous to assume that one of them would have escaped for a night on the tiles, painting the town red with an assortment of wild companions, only to return home to bed at sunrise. However, this was the last straw for Scrum and he insisted that now was the time to move them on. Or else, he said, he would release them into the wild.

This last point was enough for me to contact a local rescue centre who advertised in the yellow pages that they could "Give a Dog a Home". Tearfully, I called them up to ask if they could "Give a Mouse a Home" too and the whole sorry tale came to an end with me travelling far across town to deposit my furry brood with a local animal charity. I sent a donation several days later and received a lovely reply from the lady who ran the charity, telling me how she had fallen in love with one of the males and had kept him for herself, whilst the others had all been re-homed with little difficulty.

In addition to the little mammals and a number of tropical fish over the years, we were also given the opportunity to take on a beautiful cockatiel by the name of Spike. He had been living with a neighbour of ours for several years, but she had grown tired of the mess associated with the keeping of cockatiels as they tend to shed a fair amount of feathers and have an uncanny knack of casting empty birdseed shells far across the room with the skill of a Russian shot-put thrower in preparation for the Olympics.

Spike seemed happy enough in our house, despite being surrounded by dogs that, for the most part, left him to his own business as they got on with theirs. Exercise was something we were keen for him to have, but as we had dogs in the house we were concerned about letting him out of the cage when they were around. Our solution to this was to 'launch' him gently up the stairs, giving him the opportunity to fly around in the bedroom, bathroom and upper landing, whilst remaining safe from harm.

One day, when I was out seeing clients for work, Scrum had sent Spike up the stairs for his regular bout of exercise and had forgotten all about him whilst pottering around in his motorbike workshop out in the garden. After some time he decided he needed to use the toilet and, heading upstairs to the bathroom, he thought nothing of the fact that Barney had done his regular trick and chosen to trot alongside to accompany him.

Whilst Scrum was sitting on the loo, doing the usual 'man thing' of reading a magazine and taking his time over the whole affair, Barney wandered proudly into the room, strutting his stuff like the cat that got the cream. *Only this, instead, was the dog that got the bird!*

Nestled in his huge, staffie mouth, eyes wild with fear but beak clenched tightly closed with shock, was poor, defenceless Spike. His wonderful afternoon of free-flying fun had been rudely interrupted by Barney's decision to play 'Sylvester' to the little chap's 'Tweety-Pie'.

Scrum, after mulling over a carefully calculated decision of what to deal with first, ie, pulling up his clothing or removing the cockatiel from an incomprehensible horror, decided that Spike must be his main priority. Now, if Barney had approached *me* on that fateful afternoon, the poor bird would have been crushed to death in an instant, the second I asked the dog to release him. Barney was a complete pain for me whenever it came to trying to take things from him. In his eyes, possession was much more than nine tenths of the law and he simply wouldn't give anything away, however uninteresting said item may be perceived to be at any other moment in time.

Thankfully for Spike, Barney's reaction to his 'Daddy's' request for anything he may have was an altogether different affair and he released without question when Scrum asked him to "Give". Taking Spike gently from the jaws of death, he was placed carefully back in his cage where he appeared to be shaken but remarkably un-affected by the whole chain of events.

One day, soon after Spike's brush with death, I happened to be chatting to the neighbour he'd previously lived with and she commented upon how much she actually missed him and how she'd be happy to have him back if ever we chose to re-home him again. After some discussion we decided that Spike should go back to her, as we had the dogs and she had no other pet. As she worked full time and wasn't lucky enough to be home-based like I was, a dog was out of the question and we thought she might be lonely, so Spike could cheer her up. Little did we know that it would be HE who would be particularly cheered by moving back there.

When we carried his cage across the terrace he initially looked little concerned, despite hanging on bravely to his perch. My own interpretation of his mood was one of bored resignation - after all, life since his near death experience wasn't particularly interesting anymore. However, his reaction upon realising where he was as we placed him firmly back in the neighbour's house, was incredibly heartening as he must have suddenly remembered just how safe this old place was. We hadn't realised just how scared poor Spike must have been after his encounter with Barney and I still feel bad to think how he might have hated being with us after that.

The sound of a cockatiel singing is a beautiful thing, but none more so than the song of pure joy and relief that Spike performed that day! *He sang and sang to his little heart's content and if it could have been interpreted into English, I'm convinced he would have been voicing the 'Hallelujah Chorus' till his lungs were fit to burst!*

*As mentioned above, Barney would never give up anything to me, however boring it might have seemed. Once he had hold of it, if I wanted it there was no way he would give it up. It's therefore helpful to teach your dog a specific 'give' command to help in such situations where you need to prize your £400 smart-phone from his jaws etc.*

*Start by placing something in his mouth such as a ball, but then produce a particularly tasty morsel such as a piece of chicken. As he opens his mouth to release the ball, say "Give", or whatever command you choose, and let him have the treat. Practice this repeatedly until he will 'give' on command, however interesting the object he's got hold of.*

# Touched by a Canine Angel

At this point in time, I had believed that our 'family' was complete and no other dogs would enter our home. The balance seemed to be perfect; - an old plodder in Scrapper, a buoyant and energetic female that was Jessie and the young scamp and comedy element in Barney. But what I hadn't bargained for was Scrum's new found interest in the American Bulldog.

Before I go any further I'd like to explain that the American Bulldog is not a breed that is banned in Britain and isn't the same as an American Pit Bull Terrier which *is* illegal in the UK. Many people automatically hear the words 'American' and 'Bull' and assume that they are one and the same, but this isn't correct. American Bulldogs are a heavier and larger breed, usually predominantly white and with a less tenacious manner than the pit bull.

Their temperament is one of loyalty and strength, with just the right amount of natural curiosity to make them suitable as both family pets and household guardians. They are attractive enough to be deemed approachable by the public when at large, but fearsome enough when roused, within the confines of their own territory, to deter even the most determined criminal. They require a firm yet steady hand to ensure that their tendency towards dominance isn't allowed to unsettle the relationship from an early age and if handled correctly the bond between owner and dog can be a fulfilling and rewarding experience for both.

In the 1990's, and unlike now, American Bulldogs were both highly expensive and particularly rare. Breedings in the UK at that point had been few and far between and although they *could* be found, it was not without making a considerable dent in the pocket. In the light of this, and in an attempt to try something a little different, Scrum opted to take on a crossbreed instead. This would mean he was getting the best of both worlds as he was offered the chance to buy an American Bulldog x Dogue de Bordeaux.

Anyone familiar with the film *Turner and Hooch*, starring the actor Tom Hanks will have seen a full-breed 'Bordeaux' (aka a French Mastiff or Dogue depending on who you speak to) in full flow. My own initial reaction to the sight of that particular dog - again before my love affair with these breeds began - was one of horror and repulsion.

Wow, they could produce some slime! They're regularly seen with huge great strings of pure white mucous hanging down, almost a foot long, from each side of the heavily jowled muzzle. Whilst bubbles of snot and gunge can drip from the nostrils, huge folds of wet pink flesh will frame the enormous face and fearsome, dagger like, teeth. Very attractive indeed - *I don't think!*

What would drive anyone to want to own an animal such as that? The thought of being 'slimed' every time you hugged your dog was simply unthinkable. And this slime sticks! It's a gloopy, clingy concoction which never quite washes out of your clothes once it's welded its way onto your very best outfit. Don't even bother trying to remove it, as you will forever look as though you've lain in a garden at midnight whilst a dozen crazy snails criss-crossed their way across your favourite skirt, most expensive trousers or newly cleaned shirt.

A shake of the head can result in the ceiling looking like it's been poorly artexed as drips of drool hang down above your head. Ever threatening to drop into your eye or, worse, into your coffee! Curtains receive additional adornments in the shape of crystal droplets which may appear quite attractive until closer inspection reveals them to be pearls of mucous, deftly delivered by a sneeze from your loving canine companion. *Why on earth would I want something like THAT in my house?????*

Well, partly because it wasn't going to cost the Earth, that's why. A mere £500 - still a couple of weeks' income at least for us in those days, but it was considerably better than the £1,500 we would eventually pay for our first American Bulldog in years to come. Plus, he was with a known breeder and ready to leave his mother.

He had been "the only one in the litter and lucky to survive" - the classic 'hard luck story' which tugged at the heart strings and resulted in me relenting on the idea of yet another dog and Scrum taking a long, steady drive down to the South coast to collect our latest little bundle of joy.  And oh what joy he would be....*well, some of the time at least....*

Waiting for Scrum to arrive back from collecting the puppy, I pondered how the other dogs, particularly Barney, would respond to another member of the 'pack' being thrust upon them.  Still only just learning to understand the mentality of bull-breeds I was concerned that Barney would see the latest arrival as an immediate threat and would choose to harm the pup with no warning.  I could see how another male coming into the group could pose problems and I was also unsure of how a new addition might affect the excellent relationship between Barney and Jess.  Scrapper had remained pretty disinterested with every addition to his clan, even with regard to Jessie when they first met, but yet another male, I suspected, could prove to be too much.

However, in the early days at least, my fears would prove to be unfounded.  Scrum arrived home from his long trip South, armed with a small cardboard box - around the size of the type usually used to hold A4 copy paper.  Despite my reservations about another dog, my excitement got the better of me and, trying hard to hide my curiosity, I met him in the street as he parked the car.

Peering into the box I saw a tiny bundle of ginger/honey coloured fur and a set of bony little legs.  As I picked the puppy out of the box, still trying to fight the excitement which persisted in building up inside, the tiny little mite looked me in the eye and raised his head, exposing a smooth white neck and underbelly.  I kissed him on the chest and at that precise moment I felt an unprecedented love well up inside me.

I didn't know *why* this particular puppy had managed to get under my skin, but from that very moment I met him I had an almost instinctive feeling that my life would never be the same again. I loved each of my dogs with all of my heart, but some kind of primeval instinct drew me to this 'baby' like I'd never felt before. I immediately *knew* that this love was reciprocated and that we were absolutely, totally and undeniably meant to be together. My head was telling me that I should be angry at Scrum for wanting to bring yet another hungry belly into the house, but my heart was filled with a yearning to spend every waking moment with this puppy.

As for my concerns about how the other dogs would accept the new arrival I couldn't have been more wrong. Barney, my initial cause for concern, surprised us both with his delightful display of fatherly love for the youngster. It was like watching Jessie's response when he himself had arrived in our home and he danced around the puppy, showing his behind (a signal I now know means that he's showing that he's friendly), all the while being particularly careful not to stand on him or catch him with his mouth.

Barney offered 'play bows' with an unbelievable lightness on his feet which I had never before seen in him. He appeared to be smiling at the puppy but at no time did he actually show his teeth. Instead, there was just an obvious feeling of 'joy' about him as he realised he had a new play-mate who, for now, would have to be handled with kid gloves. Yet, it was as though Barney knew that this dog would grow into the kind of brute who would be able to take the rough and tumble games he so desired and which he played with Jessie but in a kind of reserved way, so as not to harm her delicate frame. This new boy would be able to take it like a man and Barney was ecstatic!

Again we had the name game to play and whilst sitting on my knee the puppy was subjected to a melee of majestic monikers....

Duke? (too short)

Baron? (too similar to Barney)

Tiny? (Scrum: *"Don't be so bloody stupid!!!"*)

After much consideration, I delighted in the fact that it was me who found the perfect title for my new found soul mate and he was given the name of Diesel. A name depicting power and reliability, coupled with a sense of strength that could provide a feeling of complete security. These were characteristics that he would display time and again throughout his life, but which would ultimately also play a significant part in his downfall.

And so it was that our ever increasing 'pack' became four, plus two members of the upright variety. For around 10 months everything was wonderful and they were all the best of friends. By this time Scrapper had begun to show all the signs of being an 'old dog'. The kind you see with elderly ladies, shuffling along on their way to the shops. Cloudy old eyes and crinkly grey hair giving off an image of tired wisdom not yet appreciated by their younger counterparts (*and the dogs would look something similar...boom boom!)*

Jessie had begun to slow down a little herself and although she and Barney still shared a special, almost mother & son bond, she never quite had the same regard for Diesel. They got along nicely but she didn't ever initiate play with him the way she did with Barney and he, in turn, didn't appear to be particularly interested in spending any length of time with her. As for Diesel's relationship with his staffie friend, they could almost have been termed 'partners in crime' and they often tore around the house, chasing and play fighting with a total disregard for whatever/whoever happened to be in the path of their whirlwind.

However, the most endearing relationship of all had to be the one between Diesel and me. That instinctive feeling that this was to be something special had proved itself to be right and we shared a closeness like nothing I'd ever felt before. I love my husband dearly (although I probably don't always show it too well), and the feelings I have for *all* of my dogs knows no bounds. Yet the bond I shared with Diesel was the most unconditional love I've ever experienced and, I suspect, I will never quite feel it again for any other living thing.

Although I knew he wasn't the perfect dog, in my eyes he could do no wrong at all and it was this blinkered attitude of mine that would prove to be the reason why he became such a huge problem. His behaviour would be the unexpected cause for my introduction into a whole new world of understanding how dogs think and why they do the things they do.

## The Awakening of the Beast

As soon as he was able to leave the house, we both began to take Diesel out for walks to meet the public at large. We lived in a house that literally backed onto a small park and which was a perfect place for exercising. So each day we would take all of the dogs out for walks, some together, and some on their own. As Diesel began to get bigger he would go alone as it would be difficult, particularly for me, to handle him and another dog together.

Around the eight or nine month stage in his life, he began to react differently to anything he encountered on a walk. Whether it was a person, dog, bicycle or plastic bag blowing in the wind, Diesel's predatory instincts would hit overdrive and everything became a target for his increasingly bad intentions. As he grew, so he became considerably stronger and I swear that the muscles in my arms were taking on a look favoured by Arnold Schwarzenegger and the like.

Despite the strength I needed to muster in order to hold him back if something appeared on the horizon, I never once let go of the lead. Instead I would opt to be hauled around in various directions until I would be dizzy on my feet and my hands would be raw from hanging on for dear life. As I came to realise that Diesel was becoming increasingly more menacing, I also understood that the consequences of letting go, and him actually being able to catch the object of his interest, were far too scary to contemplate.

One particular incident, surrounding Diesel and Barney, comes to mind with a mixture of horror/amusement and involved an old adversary from the days of Barney's puppy-hood.

When he was only very young, Barney had met with Connor, a border collie who belonged to our friend and neighbour, Andie. Connor was to Andie what Diesel was to me and they too shared an incredible bond which would last for many years. However, although I wasn't actually there at the time of this incident, apparently Connor had snapped at Barney whilst he was on a walk with Scrum and when he was at a very young and impressionable age. They say that an elephant never forgets, but I wonder if this very sentiment can also be applied to staffies as Barney would eventually demonstrate that, in his eyes, revenge was to be a dish best served particularly cold.

The incident happened one Saturday afternoon when I was out in the garden with Barney and Diesel. Andie walked by the gate with Connor and shouted, "Hello" so I went outside to speak to her and we chatted happily. However, without realising, I had inadvertently left the gate off the latch and a sudden gust of wind sent it blowing wide open - presenting the ideal escape route for Barney and Diesel.

In a flash, the pair of them were out of the gate and Barney, realising that before him stood his old adversary, went straight into battle mode. Whilst Andie and I looked on, bewildered at how one dog had suddenly turned into three, Barney launched himself at Connor and made an immediate aim for his face. Now whether or not Connor recognised Barney, we'll never know, but thankfully this initial bite was misdirected and allowed Connor a split second to gather his thoughts and to turn tail and run. As he headed towards the gate of his home, Barney gave chase, and Diesel went flying up the rear, eager to defend his pal and thrilled by this new game which looked, to Andie and me, to be moving towards one very unpleasant conclusion.

Before we even realised it ourselves, Andie and I were running towards her gate, speeding as fast as we could after the three dogs. At that point Andie realised that although Connor was fast enough to out-run the others, he would reach the gate and be cornered as she had actually left her house via the front door and the back entrance was locked. A huge seven foot fence surrounded her house as it was situated next door to an industrial unit and the owner of the business had paid for this security measure to protect his own premises. Although this was a wonderful boost to the safety of Andie's home, it now presented us with an impossible obstacle to overcome.

Once cornered, Connor turned to face his attackers and, with admirable confidence I had never expected to see in a collie under such extreme circumstances, he threw himself head on into the situation and stood firm, ready to fend off the beasts. As Barney tried to sink his teeth into Connors lips, Diesel arrived on the scene and began trying to join in the 'fun'. Teeth were gnashing in all directions and blood and fur were flying all around. Anyone who has been involved in this type of incident will appreciate just how noisy such situations can be and how quickly dogs can move. It is said, and I for one don't doubt it, that dogs can bite numerous times per second, with almost pinpoint accuracy.

By this time, Andie and I had reached the group and with unbelievable luck her neighbour had been in the kitchen at the rear of her house, so had heard the commotion taking place outside. She had shared access to the gate in the fence so was able to release the latch and allow Connor inside, safe from the baying hounds that wanted his blood.

Whilst Andie followed Connor inside to check on his wounds, I faced the unenviable task of trying to round up my 'monsters' who now had fire in their veins and were looking for trouble in whatever form they could find it. Barney, for whatever reason, seemed to admit defeat and headed back home to the garden. Diesel, on the other hand, was all fired up and ready for action. This incident had awoken intuitive feelings that even he didn't know he had. The American Bulldog's 'catch-dog' instinct in him was up and raring to go and he displayed the look of a teenage tearaway, seemingly strutting around the park chanting, "Bring it on, bring it on!!!"

At that moment in time, Norman, another neighbour of ours, appeared from nowhere with his old dog, Spot. This dog was around the same age as Scrapper and would never hurt a fly. Norman, too, was a gentle soul and the pair of them were simply hoping for an amiable stroll around the park, before heading home for a bite to eat and perhaps a snooze in front of the fire. Diesel, however, had other ideas.

As Diesel turned towards the two of them, I shouted to Norman, as loud as I possibly could, that he had bad intentions and would attack Spot if given the chance. Norman was amazing! With the strength and dexterity of Superman, he picked up Spot and literally threw him over a nearby wall into some unsuspecting neighbour's garden. The poor dog must have wondered what had hit him as his innocent walk in the park became a thudding landing onto some strange and unforgiving concrete yard floor.

Diesel, realising that his canine target was no longer an option, then decided to turn his attentions to Norman. If you've ever seen TV footage of a police dog demonstrating the art of Schutz-hund, you'll know just how well a 'canine copper' can target the arm of a criminal and bring him down to enable his human partner to cuff him. Well, Diesel had obviously also seen that particular piece of film and he'd studied this art with particular intent. He hurled himself at poor, innocent Norman and made a spectacular, if horrific, grab for his forearm. Thankfully Diesel had only studied this art in theory and hadn't had the opportunity to put his knowledge into practice, so his aim was fairly misplaced and he missed Norman's actual arm, but he did take a hold of the end of his coat-sleeve.

By this time I was by Norman's side and I managed to pull Diesel away whilst he made good his escape. He ran inside the yard into which Spot had been so ceremoniously dumped and swiftly closed the gate, leaving me to tackle the wild beast that was my, now almost unrecognisable, beloved canine companion.

Realising that Diesel wasn't wearing a collar, my mind was racing to find a way in which to tether him before anyone else appeared on the scene who could become another, perhaps more attainable, target of his thirst for action. I lunged at him, to try and grab his ample, semi-Bordeaux jowls and with that we both fell to the floor. Quick as a flash I pulled off my jumper, figuring that I could wrap the arms around his neck and use the garment as a make-shift lead. At that point, when it was rather too late, I realised that I was wearing nothing underneath!

And so it was that I raised myself from the floor, boobs-a-blazing for the entire world to see, and frog-marched my crestfallen pooch back to the confines of my garden. I often laugh to myself and imagine how this whole scene might have looked if a passing alien spacecraft had chosen to hover over our little field for a glimpse of life on Earth. I think that the scene which was played out that day might just have been enough to send the little green men back to their homeland with tales of how our planet was such a weird place to be that it would never be worth invading as we obviously had no intelligence whatsoever!

*Looking back at this incident, I now see that the thing which was lacking with regard to Diesel was extreme socialisation. If you choose to own a dog which packs considerable power, then you MUST socialise it as well as you possibly can. Make sure he meets all manner of things whilst he's still young and use treats to ensure that his association with EVERYTHING becomes a pleasant one.*

*If you can join a puppy training class then that's excellent (ask at your vets if you don't know where to find one as they often run these things themselves). Make sure you don't ever encourage your dog to growl at others, or at people, and when he is calm and relaxed around anything you encounter, give him gentle praise and encouragement coupled with a tasty treat.*

*Where I went wrong with Diesel is that, as soon as he demonstrated any aggression towards people/other dogs, I took him away from the situation, when I should have instead used treats and ensured a pleasant association, whilst taking him out to meet MORE strangers. Also, as he was such a strong dog, and pulling on the lead, we'd resorted to the usual choke chain which, as I'll demonstrate later on, can only serve to make the problem worse.*

## Sibling Rivalry

The clash with Connor, despite resulting in incredibly minimal damage to all concerned, had awakened something new in Diesel and from that point onwards each departure from the house into the outside world would be a battle of wills between him and us. He had developed a thirst for trouble and, being almost as heavy as me, was determined that where trouble could be had, I would, however unwillingly, have to be taken along for the ride.

His strength was increasing almost daily as he matured into a gorgeously impressive, but equally imposing animal. Therefore, to gain any control over him demanded a will of iron and a vice like grip to ensure the lead was held fast, whatever obstacle may present itself. With a fear of what might happen if I was to accidentally release him in mind, I began to read all manner of training books to find the best way to get him under control. We used broad collars, choke chains (not recommended - more on that point later), haltis and gentle leaders. None of which gave me ultimate control but some certainly allowed a degree of confidence that I could at least hold him back from anyone/thing passing by.

Walking Diesel became the ultimate chore and was no longer a pleasure in any sense of the word. Letting him run free was unthinkable, as if another dog or a person had appeared, he would have been off like a shot with the speed of a whippet and the power of a rhino. This inability to let him have fun off the lead was a particular bug-bear with me and I made it my aim to find him somewhere he could actually be allowed that freedom. Eventually we did find a secluded field with a surrounding fence and we ventured there a number of times, despite it requiring a reasonable car journey, which in itself was an event as Diesel regularly threw himself wholeheartedly into lunging at the windows whenever he saw a pedestrian.

It's quite possible that this field was, in fact, private property, but I can only be thankful that we were never disturbed and each trip was happily without incident. Looking back, even if the field had been private property, I would have readily paid any associated penalty for trespassing, just to be given the opportunity to see the joy on Diesel's face as he romped around without a care in the world.

Despite the increasing problems we encountered away from the home, up until the point when he turned around 10 months we didn't have any real problems in the house. Diesel was toilet-trained within days and had never really been a 'chewer' - *a point I'm particularly pleased about as his jaws would have made very short work of anything he'd taken a liking to.* His demeanour had always been laid back and playful and he was extremely loving to the rest of his 'family'. And to my utmost delight, it was always the case that I was the main recipient of his unconditional love.

However, at about this time - and this is something I have now experienced with many 'client dogs' - he began to change in his attitude towards Barney. Whilst they had always been the best of friends, and even, as demonstrated during the incident with Connor, 'brawling buddies', Diesel now began to show signs of much more challenging behaviour towards Barney whenever an opportunity arose. In addition, it was noted with some understandable frustration by Scrum, that it was always considerably worse when I was in the house alone with the dogs.

At the time that this began happening I had recently changed my job at The Health Scheme and I now held the impressive title of 'Account Executive' (a glorified name for a representative or salesperson if I'm honest). This meant that I was at home much more than before, as I was no longer office based and operated from a space in my bedroom which was my makeshift work-station. Working from home has both advantages and disadvantages, depending upon a person's own work ethic. It's very easy to become engrossed in breakfast television or to allow oneself an extra 30 minutes in bed before starting work in 'the office'. On the other hand, it's easy to become embroiled in your work whilst getting ready for bed, and to allow your work to encroach on your home life.

I felt I had the home-working balance about right as, being a 'morning person', I would start work around 7am creating letters and planning my day and then, appointments with clients permitting, could finish any serious work by around 4pm and begin to prepare the evening meal, whilst still being available by phone to deal with any client queries. One afternoon, I was in the kitchen doing just that when I noticed an obvious and more serious change in Diesel's behaviour around Barney. There was no particular catalyst that I could see, such as a disagreement over a morsel of food or a favourite toy, but his whole attitude seemed to switch in an instant and he could almost be seen to be 'bristling'. He was raising himself up to appear as big as he possibly could and his tail was ramrod straight, pointing menacingly to the ceiling, like a sword held aloft by an Elizabethan gentleman on the verge of taking part in a duel for the hand of the woman he loves. Yet at the same time as pointing straight up to the ceiling, his tail was quivering, almost like the rattle on a venomous snake.

The thing that I found weirdest of all was that Diesel's face seemed to change and take on an almost human expression. His face seemed to flatten and his eyebrows seemed to rise. His brow was furrowed and his mouth became almost a maniacal grin. *I'm acutely aware of how strange this will sound, but he began to look unbelievably like the actor Jack Nicholson when he starred in The Witches of Eastwick, with his knowing look towards Michelle Pfeiffer et al, giving the impression that he was about to devour them with his devilish charm!!*

Barney, in the meantime, had begun his own little show of authority and was now responding to this posturing with a stiff demonstration of what I call the *'My Dad's Bigger Than Your Dad'* display. With my complete lack of experience in all things dog, I had absolutely no idea what was going on, but I could almost feel the electricity in the atmosphere as they prepared to march into an all out battle. Within seconds (although the scene somehow went into slow motion) Diesel was snarling and snapping at Barney and the older dog was coming back at him with equal ferocity.

The noises they made and the speed at which they moved was astonishing and something I had never seen before, nor ever wished to see again. As Diesel was the bigger dog, I immediately saw him as the most likely victor in this attack so my instincts told me he had to be removed from the situation to save Barney from a likely savaging. In a show of what I now see as astounding naivety, I believed that I could prize Diesel's jaws apart, and away from Barney's flesh, with my bare hands. I stumbled towards them and placed the fingers of my right hand inside his mouth, with the sole intention of widening the cavity allowing Barney the opportunity to pull free and back away.

How wrong I was. With a power behind his jaws that could be likened to that of a crocodile, Diesel bore down with his teeth and pierced the skin of my middle and forefinger like a razor blade going through tissue paper. I felt the bones of my hand being crushed under the pressure and my head saying, *"Oh dear, that's BAD!"* Blood began to pour from my wounds as Diesel held tight until, thankfully, Barney made a new lunge for him and he released my hand as he went back to his house-mate for another bite.

Adrenaline was racing through my veins, even as their bright red contents ran down my fingers and dripped onto the carpet. It's amazing how the human mind works so illogically in a crisis and again I heard my head saying, *"That'll stain..."* with not a sensible thought of how I was going to stop the situation managing to get through the fog in my brain. Luckily another part of my conscience managed to break through to the fore and I realised that I had to get the dogs apart to prevent any further damage to either them or me.

Whether it was the fact that, despite numerous attempts to launch himself at his 'enemies' in the street, Diesel had never actually caught - or fought - anything, or whether it was Barney's shock and lack of preparation at his younger playmate's attack, I'll never really know, but thankfully neither dog appeared to have the battle skills required to follow through their bad intentions. Regardless of what happened, I was relieved at the fact that in a brief second when they were unattached to one another I managed to grab the smaller dog and hoist him skywards, before shoving him into the kitchen and securing him out of harm's way.

My hand was throbbing and I could already see that the wounds were open and sticky. No longer bleeding, but ragged and swollen, with some strange looking fatty threads hanging loose from the inside, I knew that the injury would result in a nasty scar that would be displayed, like a war wound, for many years to come. The undeniable proof that I had waded into a dog fight, like the pillock that I undoubtedly was, and confirmation that I had ended up being more injured than either of the canine participants who had each received simple scratches and scrapes.

From then on it became necessary to keep Diesel and Barney apart to prevent a repeat performance. This was no mean feat as our house was tiny, consisting of just two rooms on the ground floor and three upstairs. Looking back, I can hardly believe that we managed to keep them separate, but thanks to a regimented routine whereby each of them spent a few hours upstairs alone, before being 'rotated' and given a spell within the family fold again, we managed to avoid a repeat performance.

There was never any sign of aggression from either of them towards Jessie or Scrapper. Jess, I believe, was safe due to her gender, and Scrapper thanks to a combination of his advanced years and his lack of 'breeding equipment' as he had been neutered several years before either of them came on the scene, therefore he wasn't seen by either of them as serious competition.

Throughout the months of numerous trips to the bedroom and back again, I had little idea of the damage this would do to Diesel's already far from perfect hips. Ultimately, in the not too distant future, this, along with an even worse encounter with a far more capable adversary, would be the final undoing of my favourite ever best friend and would force me to question my motives when deciding how my dogs should live their lives.

*When two dogs begin to fight with such seriousness it's a very difficult situation for an owner and one which can all too often result in the re-homing or worse of one or the other. Firstly, it's important that owners try not to get their hands in the way as I did – believe me, it's not a pleasant experience and I was lucky that no serious damage was done to the tendons in my hand. Sometimes throwing a blanket over the dogs can disorientate them and force them apart, as can water, although as I'll recount later, this won't always work. Further on I will detail the case of two Staffordshire Bull Terriers who faced this same situation and had begun to fight. Read on to discover how the problem can be solved.*

# This One's the Real McCoy

Despite the arrival of Diesel and the fact that he was, without doubt, the most awesome of dogs, Scrum still harboured a secret desire to own a purebred American Bulldog. So, after much discussion, and the agreement that it was time to branch out into the garden and build an outdoor pen for our next arrival, the time came to purchase a wonderful boy who we proudly named Jasper.

He was fairly mature when we got him at six months old, but already he was showing signs of being an extremely handsome dog. Almost completely white with just small flecks throughout his coat and a huge dark brindle spot at the base of his tail, he cut a fine figure as he jumped up enthusiastically to greet us when we went to collect him. His manner was that of a gentle giant and he would readily sit and hand out his huge white paw as a way of saying 'Hello' whenever we would re-unite.

Although I initially found it strange having a dog that lived outside, I soon accepted that Jasper was happy there, having never lived in a house before anyway. He had a cosy kennel within a large 10ft long run and was regularly taken out for exercise and copious amounts of love and affection. In fact, it was at this point that I also discovered the joys of climbing into a dogs kennel and snuggling down in the bedding with him. *(I now regularly do this with my dogs and I like nothing better than to lay alongside them in the straw, stroking their soft fur whilst whispering sweet nothings into their big droopy ears!)*

Jasper had cost a considerable amount of money and, as such, was Scrum's pride and joy. With this in mind there was a substantial level of time and effort put into his training to ensure that he didn't develop any of Diesel's bad habits when it came to the general public. Jasper was, in fact, a whole different kettle of fish and was eager to learn and to show off his expertise when it came to walking nicely on the lead and performing simple tasks such as 'sit' etc. This fact paid off considerably during one particularly scary incident when I was taking him for a walk in the park outside our house.

As he was so well behaved around people and other dogs, I had allowed Jasper to run off-lead and we were having a whale of a time chasing around and playing hide and seek etc. Suddenly, with no clue as to where it came from, a tiny Jack Russell type female terrier appeared and began racing around Jasper, jumping in his face and generally chasing about.

I called our precious bulldog to me and, for once, he chose to completely disregard my command as he was having far more fun playing a wild game of 'chase me'. As I headed towards the pair of them, lead in hand ready to get him back under control, the terrier suddenly decided she had had enough and would prefer to head off towards another park a little farther afield. This park, however, was across an extremely busy road!

As the terrier headed for the kerb edge with Jasper in hot pursuit, I froze and watched £1,600 worth of purebred, excellent pedigree, perfectly formed American Bulldog heading for a likely collision with something fast on four wheels. My mind raced as I remembered how proudly Scrum had told his friends, family and anyone else who would listen, how he had a rare breed of dog and how wonderfully well behaved it was. With this latter thought paramount in my mind, I recalled that Scrum had told me he always used the command "Wait", rather than "Sit" when he approached a road, and how Jasper would do just that, putting his ample back-side on the floor to demonstrate just how much he intended to 'wait' for his next instruction.

I raced forward towards Jasper, shouting as loud as I could for him to "Wait!!!" My lungs were burning as my voice fought to be heard above the wind and the sound of the little terrier's excited barking as it lured my prize bulldog towards potential death. "Wait! Wait! Wait! *WAIT!!!!*" I cried, and in a memorable moment that I will cherish to the end of my days, HE DID!

Jasper stopped, dead in his tracks and sat his big, butch, beautiful backside hard down on the grass and waited there for me to collect him. The terrier speeding off across the busy road no longer interested him as some inner voice had made him listen and react to the command so regularly practiced with his 'Dad'. I've never been as proud of a dog's training as I was at that particular moment in time and it brought it home to me, rapidly, how very important such training can be.

I clipped the lead onto Jasper's collar and praised the hell out of him before walking home with my head held high and my fantastic bulldog trotting neatly beside me.

## A Millennium Gift

On the 31st December 1999 we made a decision to add to our 'family' once more. This time the plan was to obtain a friend for Jasper who was still living outside in a pen and was therefore somewhat isolated from the rest of his 'family'. This isolation was a good thing as the other 'in tact' (uncastrated) males, Barney and Diesel, didn't tolerate Jasper and his bulldog posturing at all. Scrapper and Jessie acted exactly the same towards him as they did all dogs - Jess doing her best to make friends and Scrapper simply taking no notice of him whatsoever.

After considering all manner of breeds, we happened upon an advertisement for a litter of Neapolitan Mastiffs. The drooliest of all the mastiff types and perfectly suited to outside living. We agreed we wanted a female as a male would be a recipe for disaster, but other than that we were fairly open minded in our aim as we headed to Rotherham to investigate the litter. One reason why we chose this particular sale was down to price as, having no real intentions to breed from the bitch, at just £250 the pups were an absolute steal, when other litters were being advertised at around £1,000 per puppy! Although there would be no registration papers, as the parents weren't listed with the Kennel Club, it would be possible to arrange this in the future if it were deemed necessary and upon seeing the parents it was completely obvious that they were truly pure-bred 'Neo's'.

When we first arrived we were introduced to 'mum' who, if I'm honest, didn't make much of an impression on me at all. However, with hindsight, having now bred litters myself, I understand how rearing a brood of demanding puppies can take it out of a bitch and how they tend to look saggy and worn out for quite some time after giving birth - *a bit like some humans I guess!* She was pretty enough though and the thing which struck me most was how placid and gentle she appeared to be. The couple who had bred the litter had a young boy of only around three years old and the mother of the puppies was wonderful with him so this was another bonus. Even though Scrum and I had no children of our own, there were plenty who lived around us and would play regularly on the park behind the house.

As for the father of the pups, well he was a different kettle of fish altogether. The owners had said that the mating had been accidental and whether this was true or not we'll never know. However, the sire of the pups was only about nine months old and already stood around six feet tall when up on his hind legs. He was still fairly lean, as is usual for adolescent dogs, but had the makings of a magnificent beast. Again, his demeanour was one of a gentle giant and I had no doubt at all that the puppies were from steady stock.

The lady of the house let the pups out to run around and to grant us the opportunity to pick a favourite. I'd never seen anything so cute! With their big wrinkly faces and floppy ears they were like soft, stuffed toys. Their skin was a size 16 whilst their bodies were still only an eight and as they raced around the yard they demonstrated an unanticipated level of agility coupled with an adorable, 'lollopy' gait. There were two 'blue' puppies which is an incredible grey/silver type of colour, as well as one 'mahogany' puppy which is a deep red, a little like auburn in humans, and one black/brindle female which was the same colour as the mother.

My immediate reaction was to go for one of the blues as they were almost ghost-like in their appearance and I felt they would mature into beautiful animals. The mahogany was also nice but, reminded me a little of a Bordeaux due to the colour. Much like the mother, the black/brindle didn't particularly catch my eye. However, being happy to bow to his superior knowledge of the breed in question, I again opted happily to leave the final decision to Scrum.

We enquired as to the temperament of each of the puppies and it transpired that the black/brindle one was the most outgoing and willing to stand her ground if being pushed around, whilst also being of a particularly even temperament. She was the favourite of the little boy so choosing to take her felt a bit mean, but ultimately she would be leaving anyway, so it might as well be with us. The breeders had chosen to call her Holly and she had been born on the 8th October - two days after my own birthday - making her a little lady Libra like myself.

In discussion, the breeder also mentioned that the litter were about to be featured on the BBC in an item about helping a new puppy to settle into its home. A well know canine behaviourist, Jan Fennell - aka 'The Dog Listener' was a regular contributor to the BBC's Look North local news programme and she had spent time with one of the puppies and it's new owner, demonstrating how to house-train a new dog etc. I made a mental note to watch our new girl in her soon to be aired acting debut.

On the journey home, Holly - a name we agreed wasn't particularly right in our eyes, and something we would address over the next few days - was totally well behaved, although she did manage to throw up all over me and the back seat of the car. Yet again, the once pristine interior of my lovely company vehicle was in for another soiling. It had already suffered numerous heavy vacuuming sessions in an attempt to remove the ever deepening layer of dog hairs, whilst the windows resembled smoked glass due to the thick smudges of 'snout snot' and now it had been treated to a dousing of regurgitated dog food and a thick yellow slime which would prove nigh on impossible to clean up without the feeling that I was about to add to it with the contents of my own stomach.

When we arrived home we once again had the usual introductions to go through with each of the other dogs and it was fascinating to see how, each time a new dog was introduced to the household, it would be the most recent addition that would demonstrate the greatest display of joy at the new acquisition. Just as Jessie had been overwhelmed at the arrival of Barney and he, upon greeting his now nemesis, Diesel, this time it was the latter dog who went berserk with excitement at the arrival of the little Neo lady. The big fella went crazy with delight and ran hurriedly around the room, mounting the sofa with each circuit of the lounge, before leaping off excitedly and bounding back to her for another 'Hello' sniff.

Holly, in turn, seemed just as happy as the others to be part of our ever increasing family and she also had an obvious soft spot for Diesel, so it appeared that a mutual appreciation society had been formed. The day was Millennium Eve and as the rest of the country, indeed the world, prepared to 'party like it's 1999' for the last time, we chose, instead, to spend the evening on the lounge floor, surrounded by our doggy family, watching the fireworks at the Millennium Dome on the TV as Prime Minister, Tony Blair, danced hand in hand to Auld Lang's Ayne with a most obviously, 'not amused' monarch.

Although Holly was to ultimately live outside with, or beside, Jasper, it was far too soon to expect her to be out in a pen just yet. Also, this was the middle of winter, and the prospect of putting her outside, particularly on her first night away from the litter, would not have been right. For the time being, at least, she would have to stay inside the house and Diesel would have to sleep in the lounge along with Scrapper and Jessie, whilst Barney would continue to occupy his usual spot between the two of us in our bed.

However, with the new Millennium upon us, we didn't even go to bed that night, opting instead to bring a duvet from the bedroom and snuggling down together in front of the fire. Although a very small part of me missed the opportunity to be revelling with the rest of the world, that night is etched on my heart as one of the most special times in my life.

After some consideration, 'Holly' became 'Polly' for a few hours but then, after a spoonerism meant that Scrum mixed up 'Polly' and 'Puppy', she became Poppy - and so she would remain. Poppy - my baby - in later years, my 'Bob', my 'Majestic Mamma', and my 'Boo Bar'. (Don't ask me why, they've all just seemed to suit her over the years.)

## The Tom-Boy's Troubles

From a very early age it was apparent that Poppy was going to be one of those dogs who just can't seem to help getting into trouble. I often thought that if she'd been a human she would have been a tom-boy. Much like myself as a child, (I was always the one who would go home dirty whilst my friends, who may have been in exactly the same amount of mud, grass or gravel as myself, would remain perfectly clean and shiny), Poppy seemed to attract disasters in one form or another. In fact, as she matured, she showed even greater signs of being unusually butch for a female as she even began to lift her leg whilst urinating!

Although she never quite got over the queasy reaction to travelling by car, in her youth Poppy was a regular visitor to the vets and so being transported was something she had to tolerate - *whilst I had to tolerate the cleaning up afterwards.* Neapolitan mastiffs are sometimes prone to a condition called Cherry Eye which involves the protrusion of a large pink gland that seems to almost 'pop' out from the corner of the inner edge of the eye socket.

If this condition happens in any other breed of dog, the treatment is fairly extensive and involves a general anaesthetic which is used to sedate the animal whilst the vet tucks the gland back inside the lower eyelid and stitches it closed again. A procedure that is both lengthy and expensive and when Poppy was young the cost was around £150 per eye.

However, prior to buying Poppy, Scrum had invested in an excellent book on the breed and this explained in detail what Cherry Eye was and how it should be dealt with in Neo's. Apparently, a Neapolitan Mastiff's skin is so elastic that the usual method of dealing with this eye condition isn't appropriate. Although the gland *can* be stitched back inside the eyelid, it's highly probable that the skin will simply tear and the gland will pop back out again. This in itself can cause considerable scarring and will ultimately mean that the gland has to be removed completely.

So, when Poppy's left eye 'popped' and I took her to the vets, I was pretty uncomfortable when he explained how he would operate on the problem in the widely accepted manner. I took her home from there feeling extremely uneasy and decided that further research was required to try and put my mind at rest about the impending surgery. The internet was very much in its infancy in those days and trying to find out more about the condition proved difficult. However, I am a regular reader of a monthly publication called 'Dogs Today' and this magazine included a list of people who specialised in a huge range of dog breeds.

You may wonder why I didn't simply speak to the people who had bred Poppy to find out how they had dealt with the condition in their own dogs, but they had given the impression that they actually knew very little about the breed, other than being enthusiastic owners of a pair of Neapolitans who had found themselves together one day when the bitch had been in heat. As mentioned previously, they had already declared that the breeding had been accidental and so I didn't feel that they were particularly knowledgeable of dogs at that time (having spoken to them since, their knowledge has increased considerably and they now breed prize Bordeaux). I was also concerned that they may think I was complaining about Poppy, suggesting that she was somehow 'substandard' and this was never in my thoughts at all.

Anyway, as luck would have it, the breeder listed in my magazine was also one of the most well respected producers of top level Neapolitan Mastiffs in the country. So, with my fingers crossed, I telephoned the man to see if he would be kind enough to offer me some advice. Thankfully he was home when I called as Poppy was scheduled for surgery the very next day and my anxiety was increasing by the hour. The breeder was extremely kind and helpful as he confirmed my fears that the conventional surgery for Cherry Eye wasn't suited to Neo's and that instead, the gland should be completely removed.

I explained to him that my own vet was unwilling to do this particular operation as he had told me that it could result in further complications and a condition called Dry Eye. This was where the tear duct in the eye may be affected by the removal of the gland and therefore the eye would not receive regular moisture and would require the daily application of drops or, worse still, could become infected and interfere with the dog's sight.

The breeder explained that he had bred numerous Neo's over the years, some of whom had been placed fairly high up at Crufts, and although he had done his best to breed the condition out of his dogs, in the ones where the problem had arisen he had never once had a case of Dry Eye following surgery to remove the gland. He reminded me that Neo's eyes are extremely wet and weepy anyway, simply by their natural make-up, and so there was usually an excess of moisture available. If this tear supply were to be affected by the removal of the gland, there should still be sufficient production to moisturise the eye to a similar level of any other breed of dog.

What he then said was extremely helpful and went very much above and beyond the call of duty as far as I was concerned. He told me that his own vet would be able to remove the gland under a simple local anaesthetic and that the cost was only £40 per eye. In addition, he said that it wouldn't be unrealistic for his vet to believe that I had purchased Poppy from him, as he was less than 100 miles away from where I lived and people had been known to travel much further to obtain a pup from one of his breedings. In which case, he told me I should contact his vets and ask to have the procedure on Poppy, but under his registration, and then I would pay the bill myself.

This was excellent news and really put my mind at rest. I determined that I would speak to my own vets in the morning and would cancel Poppy's surgery in favour of this alternative procedure at the breeder's vets. Although this would entail an increased amount of travelling, a thing which Poppy wouldn't like at all, it would also save me in excess of £100 and a considerable amount of concern over whether or not her eye was going to be right.

The next morning I booked Poppy in for surgery at the other vets which was based in Boston, Lincolnshire. I lived in Hull so, as previously mentioned, there would be a fair bit of travelling involved. In light of this, the vet I spoke to asked me whether or not Poppy's other eye had yet 'popped'? This took me aback a little as it hadn't occurred to me that it was so common as to affect both eyes, but apparently this would more than likely be the case.

He suggested that perhaps I would like to wait until the second gland appeared so that he could carry out the procedure on both at the same time, to help reduce my travelling. After a couple of days, when nothing had happened with the second one, I went ahead and booked her in anyway, as I was concerned that the original gland was rubbing on her eyeball causing her some discomfort.

The removal of the gland was unbelievably swift and simple and produced very little blood at all. Poppy seemed fairly unconcerned after the procedure and we headed off home again. That night I was a little bit worried that she may be in some pain, but a call to the vet reassured me that she would be fine and I went off to bed, leaving her to sleep off her queasiness after the journey and to reflect on the day's events. *The next morning, almost as though 'The Lord Sod' himself had visited upon us to administer his very typical law, up popped the other gland!!!*

Within days of the second eye being operated on and life beginning to get back to normal again without any more sickly trips in the car for Poppy, she was playing in the garden when I noticed a significant pool of blood spreading out from around her front paw. On closer inspection, she had a really nasty split deep into the pad of one of her toes and blood was coming out pretty thick and fast. So, yet another trip to the vets - the local one this time at least - resulting in a heavy sedation and a number of stitches, protected by an enormous pink bandage which Poppy delighted in chewing at every opportunity.

One afternoon we were in the garden and she was running around in the gap between the perimeter fence and Scrum's workshop-cum-shed. The end of this gap, which was a kind of narrow corridor, was sectioned off by an ornate wrought iron gate topped with attractive arrow head features. Poppy had a habit of putting her front paws on the middle section of the gate whilst she watched what was happening beyond there, but she wasn't normally wearing a huge bandage.

Thus, true to form, with her accident prone track record, she proceeded to wedge the bandage (and the paw within) between a metal upright section of the gate and the blunt side of an arrowhead. This resulted in her getting stuck to the gate and howling the place down until I could get to her and try to release the paw.

Before I had the opportunity to do just that, she'd pulled herself backwards, away from the gate, and all that remained was the now detached bandage, still wedged in the iron, whilst she bounced around the garden with her stitched paw paddling through the puddle of urine freshly produced by Jasper through the meshing on his pen! So, another trip to the vets, another car 'clean up job' and yet another excessive bill for a further bandage and consultation to check her paw. Poppy cost me hundreds over the years, but was worth every single penny and more to boot.

One of her last ever visit to the vets involved me having to roll up my sleeves and play surgery nurse as we attended fairly late in the day to check out what I had assumed to be the sudden appearance of a cataract. Although I appreciated that Poppy was getting on in years, I was surprised at how quickly her eye had clouded over as I'd been under the impression that cataracts developed fairly slowly. However, it was in the depths of the winter months, one weekend, that I noticed this. During the working week I would only see Poppy, and my other dogs that lived outside, during the hours of darkness, and then lit only by dim electric lighting.

I noticed Poppy's eye had turned milky in appearance on the Saturday morning of the weekend, but we were expecting a litter of puppies from another female at any moment soon, so I decided her trip to the vets could wait as the problem wasn't a particular 'emergency', although I did understand that cataracts could be a sign of other, more serious problems, such as diabetes. However, she hadn't been drinking or urinating any more than usual, so I didn't think this was due to anything other than her ever advancing years.

When I finally got her to the vets on the Monday evening, I was full of shame following the actual diagnosis. When the vet took a proper look at Poppy's eye, he physically recoiled in horror as he exclaimed that this was no cataract, but that it was, in fact, a huge ulcer on her eyeball, caused by some kind of grassy foreign object. (I would regularly allow Poppy to roam around the garden to potter around and simply sniff the grass or lie in the sunshine and I can only assume that she had brushed against a bush, or branch, and this had caught her eyeball, causing some foreign matter to be left behind and the eye to ulcerate.) I felt absolutely terrible for not taking her to the vets as soon as I'd noticed the eye, but it was a genuine, if horrible, mistake.

As this was now early evening, the nursing staff had left for home and so the vet had to sedate Poppy and the two of us sat cross-legged on the floor as he first removed the offending piece of greenery, and then, after 'flushing' the eye to remove any further debris, or potential infection, he had to stitch her eye closed whilst I helped with the pointing of a special light and holding the head in position. He had asked me if I was squeamish, but I explained that if it was to help my dog, I would cope with anything.

*What I did find strange was that the scene brought back memories of a particularly scary TV programme I had seen in my youth, presented by the then 'Dr Who', Tom Baker. It had been a series of horror stories, read by him in a kind of adult version of the early evening children's programme, Jackanory. I remember feeling particularly grown up as the series was shown around 10.30pm, just after Christmas one year and I had just received my first portable television as my main festive gift. This meant that I could now watch TV in my own room, as late as I liked and whatever channel I wanted - bearing in mind that in those very early days there were only THREE to choose from.*

*As the credits rolled at the end of the programme, a sequence of paintings were shown and one of these involved a doll with its eyes stitched closed. Very strange indeed, and a morbid demonstration of how impressionable children can be when we consider that the image has stayed with me for over 30 years. When I think how scary it was in black and white, I'm thankful that my parents hadn't been well off enough to buy me a colour set!*

However, the actual procedure carried out by the vet was surprisingly interesting to watch, and didn't concern me, or upset me at all. To ensure the eye didn't close too tightly as a result of any swelling, the vet also included in his stitching, a small, purple plastic bead. After several days of struggling with the necessary 'Elizabethan Collar' (a flexible plastic cuff which is placed around the dog's neck after surgery, to ensure she couldn't touch the wound with her paws, or anything else for that matter), Poppy managed to free herself from its restrictions and pulled it off altogether. This gave her the opportunity to scratch at the eye and, whilst out of our sight, remove the stitching and allowing the lid to open.

Thankfully, the eyeball itself had begun the clear up nicely and there was no obvious scarring to the eye. In addition to this, in a stroke of luck for Poppy, it would seem that there had been no lasting damage to her sight as she could follow my hand with the eye when I waved it in front of her. However, there was still one little problem and that was with the purple plastic bead. Although the eye was now open, the bead remained stitched to her 'eyebrow' so that she resembled some kind of ageing punk rocker with a rebellious piercing. This stayed in place for some time until, I assume, the stitches dissolved as they should have done and the bead dropped off, never to be seen again.

## Poppy Cleans Up

Probably the most scary, amusing and memorable incident to happen with Poppy involved an extremely old, cylinder vacuum cleaner I had. I'd guess she will have been between four and five months old at the time and I'm amazed the experience didn't scar her for life.

I was cleaning the house one sunny afternoon and Jessie was lazing on the sofa whilst Diesel was wandering around in the garden. Poppy was simply doing what pups do by taking an intense interest in my actions and, whilst not actually interfering as such, she was following the sweeping head of the vacuum with her nose and just generally being a nuisance (but in the nicest possible way).

Noticing that the suction on the vacuum had reduced considerably since I'd first started on the lounge carpet, I turned off the machine using the button on the side and opened up the end of the cylinder to take out the dust-bag, in order to empty it out and revitalise the suction of the machine.

Now I'm not sure whether I'm the type of person who is highly 'magnetised' or if I'm just unbelievably unlucky, but electrical goods simply don't seem to agree with me. I've lost count of the number of washing machines I've had since leaving home, but I would guess it's at least a dozen.

After managing to destroy an ancient free standing washer and separate 'spinner' I then progressed onto a series of twin-tubs with varying degrees of success. The most memorable of these was given to me by my Gran who had finally succumbed to the modern age and taken on board an automatic machine.

At the time that I was given this washer we were living in a small, rented, house and since moving there, I had noticed that the microwave had begun to give off the occasional small shock (much the same as the static experienced by some people when getting out of a car). I hadn't been too perturbed by this, as I had always suffered with static and, again, was putting this down to me being 'highly charged' or some such thing.

One afternoon whilst doing the laundry, I unplugged the microwave to use the socket for the washing machine and filled it with hot soapy water up to the brim. I began to clean dirty tee-shirts and underwear etc, happily day-dreaming about something or other, whilst Scrum was sitting in the other room, watching the TV.

For anyone not familiar with the old twin-tub machines, the rinsing action was done by placing the clothes inside the 'spinner' section and then pouring fresh water over them. When the lid was closed, this would set the machine spinning and, with the aid of centrifugal force, the dirty water would be pushed out of the outlet tube and into the sink.

However, this time as the spinning section of the machine fired into action, the outlet pipe slipped off the sink and fell to the floor, creating a huge, and ever increasing, puddle of dirty, soapy water. Not noticing this, I was resting my hands on the edge of the machine and was steadily being surrounded by the water, which in turn formed some kind of electrical circuit - with me as the earthing point - *and I found myself being shocked through from head to foot, whilst at the same time being unable to free my hands from the machine as the force of the electricity had made them stick solid to the stainless steel surface!!*

I was also not able to shout as I was paralysed by the shock and my head was racing with the most ridiculous ideas. *You may recall how I had discovered that lucid thought can become impossible in times of crisis, such as during the fight between Barney and Diesel? Well, the uppermost thought that ran through my mind at this particularly scary time was, "Why would my Gran be trying to kill me???!!" How strange is that?*

After what felt like an eternity, but what was probably only seconds, I managed to think straight again and realised that I had to free myself from the current. I kicked out at the outlet pipe to stop the puddle from growing any deeper and then, using all the strength I could muster, I flung my hands upwards and outwards away from the machine and managed to make good my escape.

Soon afterwards I asked my brother to check the electrics in the house as he is a qualified electrician. He found that the whole wiring system was mixed up and upon checking the fuse box he discovered that one of the fuses had been armed, not with thin and easily burned out fuse wire, but a great thick lump of copper cable! He reckoned that in the event of an appliance needing to blow this fuse, its inability to do so could have resulted in the whole house burning down.

Needless to say, I now have the greatest respect for electricity, but this hasn't meant that electrical goods have the same level of respect for me. Hence, in addition to the numerous washing machines, music systems and televisions that have shared my life, there have also been a considerable number of vacuum cleaners. In fact, at this very moment of writing, I currently have six (yes, SIX) 'dead' machines dotted around the house as I am once again having to clean my floors with a small hand-brush and accompanying shovel, since yet another 'Hoover' has, quite literally, bitten the dust!

I keep the old machines as a 'parts warehouse' so that when my latest one 'dies' there's a possibility that I may have a part from another to fix the problem. I've even managed to kill a Dyson - considered to be the Rolls Royce of the carpet cleaning world - so I suppose I'm something of an expert now.

However, in going back to the story of Poppy, this may go some way to explaining why I was using such an ancient machine, as I had managed to finish off everything else I'd owned and had happened upon this one. My friends and family are aware of my electrical affliction and so I seem to be the first one they think of when getting rid of any old appliances.

So, as I was removing the dust-bag from the cylinder vacuum to empty it and increase the suction, I stood the machine on its end, opened up the flap into which the suction tube fits and removed the bag, leaving the machine standing upright with the empty compartment facing the ceiling. I headed for the dustbin in the garden and, expecting Poppy to do her usual trick of following my every move, left the back-door open so that she could do just that.

However, on this occasion, Poppy had something far more interesting than little old me to catch her eye and as I glanced into the lounge I saw her approaching the now silent vacuum, so that she could take a closer look. Peering into the open cavity where the dust-bag would normally sit, she decided that she couldn't quite see what went on inside and her naturally youthful curiosity took over, so that she actually placed her head deep down inside the open cylinder of the machine.

At this point I was smiling to myself and thinking what a sweet little pudding she was, when she decided she'd seen enough and lifted her head up to check out something else. The only trouble was, being a Neapolitan Mastiff, and with a neck that's covered in numerous folds of skin resembling a slouching sock, her head had other ideas. As she lifted her face skywards, the vacuum cleaner remained firmly in place and lifted with it. Gravity then took a good strong hold of the machine and pulled it further down her neck until her whole head was buried deep inside the belly of the monster!

As would be expected, this totally freaked Poppy out, and she began to panic at the feeling of being attacked by this once friendly looking animal. She started to jump around, bucking and shaking her head, trying to release the vacuum from her rapidly swelling neck. At this point Diesel, who had been mooching around in the garden, was suddenly on full alert at the sight of this alien creature darting around the lounge. No longer did he recognise the 'beast' as his little pal Poppy, and instead saw a raging monster, hell bent on taking over his hard-won territory. As he raced towards Poppy, my frozen statue of a body finally sprung into action and I chased after him to catch hold of his collar before he could throw himself upon her helpless frame.

After quickly dragging a snarling and snapping Diesel back into the garden and locking the door to keep him out, I turned my attention to Poppy who was still thrashing around madly. My biggest concern was that she would break her neck with the force with which she was banging into the surrounding walls and furniture, including most alarmingly, a glass fronted cabinet. *But this crashing into objects was nothing compared to what happened next....as she banged into the wooden fire surround, the button on the machine depressed and, due to the fact that the vacuum cleaner was still connected to the mains, the 'monster' began to fight back, letting out a deafening, relentless 'moan' that filled poor Poppy's ears with sound and her heart with terror.*

Fearing that the suction fan inside the machine may be close to Poppy's face, with the potential of slashing into her little black puppy nose, I wrenched the plug from the wall and the machine's wailing was silenced. This, however, had not been done soon enough to prevent Poppy's bowels from choosing to empty themselves across the whole of the lounge, spurred on by the enormous panic of the situation and opting to spread their contents far and wide, filling the room with the stench of panic.

Poppy continued to charge around, bearing into anything and everything that happened to be in her way, but I finally managed to grab the machine and hold it still. Throughout the whole course of events, Jessie had stood calmly on the sidelines watching the situation unfold without even a flicker of concern for either one of us. Unlike Diesel, she didn't see the 'monster' as a threat to the household. She simply saw Poppy with a vacuum cleaner on her head, dancing around the room like a dog possessed! *I'm sure she must have found the whole thing highly amusing and later recounted the story to Scrapper with great delight. He, however, lay sleeping upstairs throughout, and remained totally oblivious to the huge excitement which unfolded beneath him.*

I gently pulled the vacuum cleaner down to floor level and Poppy, however reluctantly, had to go with it. I then sat on the cylinder to prevent her from thrashing around any further, whilst she lay on her stomach at the end of the machine. I could hear her terrified breath gushing from her mouth and my head was spinning as I considered my next course of action.

I could see on the top of the cylinder, which was now resting on Poppy's shoulders, there were two small screws which, I guessed, must be holding the top of the machine in place. If I could remove these, although it would result in Poppy have a plastic collar around her neck which would have to be tackled separately, it would at least mean that she could see and breathe properly. So, trying to convince her to 'stay', I made a mad dash for the kitchen to grab a knife from the cutlery drawer which could be used as a make-shift screwdriver and remove the 'cuff' from the top of the vacuum.

As I came back into the room at lightening speed (not bad for little old me, who can't run to save her life) Poppy was just beginning to rise again, so I grabbed her and managed to ease her down once more. Trying to reassure her while my hands shook fiercely, I slowly but surely managed to get the screws to turn and remove them from the machine. Now, all I had to do was pull off the 'cuff' at the top and she'd be free, so with one big tug....

Nothing! The 'cuff' remained stuck solid and it turned out that the screws must have had some other purpose, but either way, the thing still remained steadfastly around her neck. Thoughts of the fire brigade and having to take her to the vets with the vacuum still in place whizzed through my mind, but I managed, thankfully to grasp a single, sensible thought and realised that 'what goes on, must come off'.

Taking a firm, yet gentle, hold of the flesh surrounding Poppy's chin, I gradually eased the folds of skin back out of the entrance hole to the cylinder. By taking things steady and remaining calm, the fur of her neck was slowly released and I was able to pull the machine from her head with a considerable 'POP'. Her eyes were wild and bulging and her mouth and chin were covered in hot, sticky foam, but thankfully there were no cuts to her skin and no damage to her teeth or tongue.

Poppy had survived probably the most traumatic event of her life thus far, and one of the most horrendous (yet shamefully amusing) of mine. After speaking to the vet to ensure that she didn't require any treatment, Poppy was left to recover in peace and she slept for almost twelve hours solid.

This latest incident confirmed to me that we had definitely found a highly accident prone dog. Only a week later in the local press there was a feature on a puppy that had put its head through the wheel of a small, Lambretta type scooter, and the owner had needed to call the fire brigade to remove the offending object. Thankfully we'd managed to sort out our own dilemma without their help, but it's certainly another of those stories to be shared with friends when in need of a smile.

## Cereal Killer

As Poppy matured I began to make exactly the same kind of mistakes with her as I had made with Diesel and she began to get huge ideas, way above her station. She was a massive part of my world and I completely idolised her in the same way that I did 'my boy'. This did her no favours and she began to cling to me in a way that wasn't particularly healthy for either of us.

At the time, I hadn't even begun to study dog behaviour so my way of dealing with any problems was completely wrong. Although it was also the way in which countless other owners react when things go awry. Poppy's immense attachment to me began to manifest itself in a severe case of 'Separation Anxiety' which, I now know, is what can happen when the dog feels so desperate at being left without her owner and, if left alone, she cannot cope - and this feeling of increasing anxiety then results in bad behaviour such as soiling, chewing, howling etc. Poppy's reaction to separation anxiety was to do each of the above!
I would regularly come home from work to find a huge pile of faeces on the kitchen floor (believe me, when a Neo 'goes' it goes big style), usually accompanied by a puddle of urine. In addition, she would have wrecked her bed, along with anything else she could get hold of. On one particular occasion I came home from work and as I entered the kitchen I could hardly believe the scene of devastation that I met. The floor was covered in a gloopy white substance that felt 'grainy' underfoot and which stuck to everything it encountered.

Upon closer inspection I realised that Poppy - always a smart cookie (although I suspect this was luck rather than judgement) - in this instance had surpassed herself. She had opened the fridge to take out the milk and mixed it carefully with a huge bag of porridge oats from the cupboard, to create a tasty snack!! I also left her alone for only a short while one morning and when I returned she'd eaten a whole bag of frozen chicken fillets which were thawing on the kitchen side for our dinner.

My reaction to the problem was both totally wrong and equally common, but of course at the time I thought it was the right thing to do. Whenever I got home to some kind of destruction or a puddle etc, I would shout at Poppy and drag her over to the offending mess to remind her just how bad a dog she really was. In addition to this, whenever I had to leave her alone, we would go through a ridiculous parting ritual which consisted of me securing the now necessary padlock which was attached to the fridge, placing paper on the floor to catch the mess and moving anything 'chewable' onto the back of the work surfaces to try and make it out of reach - not easy when you're dealing with a Neapolitan mastiff, standing five feet tall on her hind legs.

A further, elaborate step I took - and one which, at the time, I felt was genius, was to remove the drawers from their rails in the kitchen units and then tie the lower cupboard doors together using string and a couple of hooks I had screwed to the insides, before replacing the drawers. All of this would be done in full view of Poppy, whilst throughout I would be sternly reminding her how she was to behave herself and not mess in the house because, "Good girls go outside to wee wee and Mammy won't be long...blah, blah, blah..."

All that this routine served to do was make Poppy acutely aware of the fact that, once again, she was going to have to cope with being left alone. This, in turn, meant that by the time I left the house, her anxiety levels were at fever pitch and she simply HAD to do something to take her mind off the isolation.

In desperation, after weeks of coming home to mess and destruction, we decided that Poppy could stay outside whilst we were at work and Scrum put his joinery skills to good use and made her a huge kennel. It was so big I could easily fit inside with her and regularly did so for a cuddle. However, when she was initially left she wasn't happy and I remember coming home on the first day we'd left her outside to discover that she'd decided she was coming in whether we wanted her there or not. As I walked into the house and through to the kitchen, peeping through a huge hole in the back door was Poppy's cheeky face!! *I was only thankful that I hadn't been much later as if she'd managed to get here entire head through, we could have had a repeat of the vacuum cleaner experience with some pretty nasty results!*

*Looking back, my reaction and way of dealing with Poppy's behaviour was classic for the situation and something I have encountered numerous times with my business. Later on I'll explain what SHOULD have been done and how owners can deal with this particularly stressful problem. I will also recount how one of my very first clients called me with this exact type of dilemma and how the excellent results encouraged me to believe that I DID actually know what I was talking about.*

Sadly, although Poppy was still very much alive when I started this book, she is now no longer with us, although she made it to 11 years old, which for a Neapolitan mastiff is amazing. She gave birth to 16 puppies throughout her life, from only two litters. This in itself, although quite a feat, is shown to be all the more remarkable when I say that the first litter consisted of just one dog and one bitch - the rest came in a second litter, via a labour lasting 24 hours and that included two 'blue' coated puppies. One of these was born in the field next to our house when I'd erroneously thought, after the tenth arrival, that Pop had finished giving birth to her entire litter and so had taken her outside to relieve herself. This little outing finished up with me running along behind her - brand new, mucous covered pup in hand, and with her sashaying nonchalantly back to the house as though this was an everyday occurrence.

Two of her second litter were born dead, one after the other, and at that point I presumed that she must finally be at the end of her labour. However, she gave birth to one final puppy, around the 24 hour mark, which I gently handled and removed the membrane from its mouth, just in case there could be the slightest glimmer of life.

*And there was....with a huge gasp followed by a newborn squeak, the final puppy took hold of life and began to wriggle around in my hands. I actually find birthing puppies quite stressful as I worry about the way the mothers will tug at the umbilical cord and it makes me pretty squeamish, but it's a fantastic thing to behold when a tiny puppy breathes its first breath.*

I'm sure that becoming a grandmother is a wonderful thing and being a mother, even more so. Yet, throughout my own life, never having had a human child of my own and instead opting for the four legged variety, nothing can compare with the pride of helping my beloved canine companion to deliver her brood, and to show her just how special she was at this time by lavishing her with love. Poppy was a fantastic mother and in spite of her size, showed the agility and poise of a prima ballerina whilst tiptoeing around her huge litter. She was always tolerant of the undoubted pain of feeding, particularly as the puppies grew teeth, and she would reprimand them in a firm but fair manner.

Poppy was my one remaining link to Diesel and I dreaded the day when she would no longer be by my side. Thankfully I have two of her beautiful offspring – her son, Tucker and daughter, Ripley. They each bring me enormous joy with the way they look at me, displaying the same cheeky glint in their eyes as their incredible mother. And the way that they utter the exact same mournful wail, almost coming from depths of the soul, when they want my attention, can often seem like 'my girl' is still here.

Thankfully, Poppy's end was swift and painless - free from her usual 'accident prone' manner- and leaving me only with happy memories of our wonderful time together. *I loved you Poppy and I know, without doubt, thanks to your regular demonstrations of unconditional and unwavering affection, that you loved me too. (Of course, I know she's not reading this - more of that type of thing to come – but she's in my heart and I know her spirit remains with me always.)*

Soon after Poppy's death I was given a pup that had been fathered by one of her sons so I now have her granddaughter in the form of Blossom. She's a gorgeous little dog who's not overly droopy in the eyes and has that same cheekiness about her that I love. However, I've no plans to breed her and so the line will no doubt stop with her, but as she came along so soon after I lost Pop I feel she was sent to me to help heal the sadness in my heart, and she's certainly done that.

# A Thirst for Knowledge Begins

*"He's at it again, that b****y dog of yours!!"* said the voice at the end of the line.

This would be the statement that would force me to reconsider my situation and realise that I HAD to take steps to change Diesel's behaviour. At the time I wouldn't know it, but the fact that he had now begun to make Scrum the object of his aggression would be the thing that made me see that some kind of behavioural modification was not only possible, but it had now become vital and that it was also way above my own capabilities.

We had always known that he was a problem when out in public, and for quite some time now we had been keeping Diesel away from Barney in fear of the consequences, but with both my husband and I he had always been the perfect dog. Things went wrong when Scrum had to go away with work and throughout the fortnight we spent without such an obvious 'master' in the house Diesel was to be promoted beyond recognition thanks to my very own total naivety.

As he was the epicentre of my world, the minute I got out of bed my thoughts would turn to my favourite dog. However unfairly it may now seem, in an evening he would undoubtedly spend considerably more time with me than upstairs in enforced isolation, whilst the lovely Barney (who at the time, I'm ashamed to say, I considered to be 'public enemy number one' following his fight with Diesel) would be sent to Coventry - otherwise known as the bedroom, so that I could be spend time with the one who had become my main priority in life.

If I happened to be watching the TV and sitting in a chair, Diesel would come up and request a cuddle. This I would give, without question, and if he then began to climb up onto the chair to sit with me, I would jump off and sit on the floor - allowing him to take over the more comfortable spot - after all, he was 'my boy' and who wants to have a huge mastiff sitting on their knee, *so it made perfect sense (didn't it???)*

When I left for work each morning, Diesel would be left upstairs in the main bedroom. In fact, more than that, he would be left on the bed. Okay, let's be honest, even more than that, he would often be left snuggled up, under the duvet, surrounded by his toys and with the portable television chattering away to itself, just to ensure he wasn't bored!

I worryingly recall how the window cleaner once arrived to clean the upstairs windows whilst I was at work, and obviously disturbed Diesel from his comfy slumber. The poor man's face, when he came to collect the payment, as he recounted the terror he had experienced when Diesel had launched himself at the flimsy glass window, was unforgettable. I'm eternally grateful that he didn't fall off his ladder, as I'm sure that would have resulted in a visit to the Court for me plus a decidedly one-way trip to the vets for my dog.

All of this fawning behaviour on my part was gradually eroding any respect that the dog may have had for his owners. Of course, he idolised his Mam and would never hurt her as she was the alpha female who would fit nicely with his aspirations of being the alpha male. However, until Scrum, the existing boss of this outfit, had gone away, Diesel had happily accepted a more submissive role in the 'pack'. Now though, a combination of my relentless adoration for the dog, coupled with the fact that the only serious contender for the 'top dog' position was currently absent from the equation, only served to convince Diesel that he could become the only one to give orders to his pack-members. However wrong this may have been, he was  the one who could demand to be obeyed, and I would do the obeying.

As I regularly say, the trouble with dog training is that *everybody* is an expert. There is SO much information bandied about and, as a totally clueless owner, I understandably struggled to know what was right and what was wrong. Add to this the fact that dog training has evolved beyond recognition in recent years, even though there are ancient books which still remain on library shelves and the whole issue becomes a minefield.

When I was in my early teens the buzz in the dog training world came from a lady called Barbara Woodhouse. This bossy, yet rather prim, elderly lady encouraged everyone to use a choke chain and to virtually bully the dog into submission. Yes, it worked in many cases, but only because I now understand that the poor dog was too terrified to do anything other than what was being bellowed into its ear.

To demonstrate my point of how methods can differ entirely, I recall visiting a training class with a view to taking Poppy along when she was just a pup. I knew enough at that point to realise that it was a good idea for owners go along and check out trainers and their classes before actually committing to anything, so off I went (minus a dog) to observe what went on. The training was taking place in two separate rooms and the first one I entered contained a class being run by a chap who I took an instant dislike to. I wasn't exactly sure why I didn't like him, but I've always trusted my instincts on this type of thing and there was just something about his manner that made me uncomfortable.

This man stood rigid at the front of the class, almost like a tyrannical sergeant major in charge of a troupe of soldiers. He took a beautiful Belgian Shepherd from its owner and walked him into a space at the end of the room, in order to demonstrate how to teach a dog to 'down' (i.e. lie flat on the floor). Taking a firm hold of the lead he yelled at the dog to "Down". Nothing happened so he repeated the command even louder whilst simultaneously jerking the lead to remind the dog that HE was in charge of the situation. The dog (probably by now wondering what the hell this idiot was shouting about as the word 'down' meant nothing to him) still remained standing.

At that point the imbecile *(note to reader: I had to work incredibly hard not to write the word that was REALLY in my head here, but I understand that there could be children present)* bent down and trod HARD on the lead, close to the end of the dog's choke chain and slammed the poor, defenceless animal's head down to the floor, forcing him to 'down' whether he'd wanted to or not.

I could sense the air of discomfort which descended upon the room and the owner of the Shepherd glared at the so called 'trainer' questioningly. "Don't worry" said the idiot, "Trust me - I'm a dog trainer". *At which point I struggled hard to contain my reaction in wanting to shout, "No, trust ME mate, you're a w****r!!!!" Needless to say, I wasn't going to take my precious dog to THAT particular class.*

Thankfully, the second room was a totally different experience and I thought it particularly strange how two people could be working under the same roof, as part of the same training club, but be using such completely opposite methods. This class was being run by a lady called Karen and she had as her 'demonstration model' a cute miniature poodle wearing a pink, diamond studded collar. Karen used the kind of methods that I would want to use on Poppy and included plenty of treats and gentle coaxing, rather than heavy handed bullying. It was thanks to this that I happily went ahead and arranged to join the class the following week.

So, having highlighted how there can be so much information available when trying to train a dog, I decided that the only way I could be sure of sorting Diesel out would be by enlisting the help of an expert in canine behaviour. With this in mind, my first port of call was the vets to find out if they had anyone in particular who they could recommend, to help me bring my dog down a peg or two. The vets suggested I call a lady who was a member of C.O.A.P.E which stood for the Centre of Applied Pet Ethology. Very grand indeed!

However, when I called the lady to discover more about her service I was horrified (and disappointed, in view of the seriousness of my need) to find that behaviourists of her type charged an average of £80 per hourly session and, knowing Diesel like I did, I anticipated this would mean *many* expensive hours. Although both Scrum and I were working, this still felt like a huge amount of money and the lack of any guidance on how many hours would be required meant that I simply daren't commit to such a course of treatment.

After many calls to various behaviourists around the country (in the vain hope that someone might just give me all of their knowledge for free), I eventually happened upon a lovely lady called Deborah Bragg who ran an organisation called The Canine Behaviour Centre. She was based quite a long way from Hull so, after listening patiently to my story about how Diesel had changed from being just a 'monster' into a 'Dad hating monster', she explained that due to the distance she didn't see me as a viable client. Thankfully though, she then went on to say that she ran a correspondence course in Canine Psychology and that she would (kindly) recommend some changes I could make in my behaviour towards Diesel and if I noticed an improvement, perhaps I would like to enrol on the course?

*And that, dear reader, is how one's life can change in an instant! I had no idea how much this would affect my future and the fascinating world this would open up for me. A new day had definitely dawned....*

For the next few days I stuck rigidly to the instructions Deborah had given me and I ensured that Scrum did exactly the same. Less than a week later we had both begun to notice a marked improvement in his whole attitude towards us and, in particular, in his lack of aggression towards Scrum. This, in turn, served to demonstrate to me that we humans could, in fact, 'talk to the animals' even if it was done using no words and only body language and attitude, but it was more than enough to convince me that I needed to enrol on the canine psychology course and I could feel myself becoming drawn into this strange new world of dog behaviour.

Around this time there was a television programme being shown on the BBC called 'Barking Mad' and this was a much updated version of the old series featuring Barbara Woodhouse. However, this programme showed just how much dog training had changed and the methods used on here were totally different to the old fashioned 'bossing' behaviour. *Plus, there wasn't a choke chain in sight!* One of the trainers featured on this show was a lady called Sarah Whitehead and I noted with interest that she also wrote for a monthly magazine I read called Dogs Today. I'd seen that Sarah ran a number of courses through The Animal Care College based in Ascot and again, these were undertaken via correspondence and backed up by 'practical weekends' where appropriate.

I can understand how people may wonder how someone can be taught to train a dog when there isn't actually any 'hands on' practical work, other than a few days throughout the whole of the course. However, the training is designed to teach the theory behind the whole idea of dog behaviour and, if I'm brutally honest, it isn't until someone feels brave enough to actually launch themselves into the real world (or if they spend their life around dogs, perhaps as a kennel hand or as a breeder etc) that anything is truly learnt.

Someone who is a product of one of these courses will almost certainly know immeasurably more than the average dog owner, but one thing I have come to learn over the years is that there is no substitute for actually trying the different techniques on dogs to find out what works best. There are no guarantees in dog training and what works well with one dog can leave another almost laughing at you, *as if to say, "Is THAT it???"* Through a system of trial and error I have come to know what it most *likely* to work for any particular problem, but this is still not a certainty and it can require another approach.

However, throughout my training period I studied hard and, if I'm honest, although I learnt a lot I was still pretty poor at putting it into practise with my own dogs. Scrum still maintains that my own group of canine chums are hardly trained at all and I have to concur. *I like to see it a little bit like the plumber's tap being the one that drips!*

Most behaviourists will tell you that it's difficult to handle their own 'doggy dilemmas' as they feel way too close to the situation and I must admit I'm inclined to agree. I recall having a bit of a heated discussion with one of my behaviourist friends who was trying to advise me which of my two males I should have neutered and I was convinced at the time that she was wrong. In hindsight, I'll admit that I can now see she was most probably right, but my pride got in the way and I stupidly couldn't see 'outside the box'. *(So, Jenny, if you're reading this – sincere and heartfelt apologies and I really hope life's good for you. x)*

Time is a very precious commodity and one which is put to better use making the lives of other dog owners easier. My own dogs don't currently cause me any particular problems, but if they ever begin to, I'll know just how to deal with them.

From the beginning of my 'awakening' I completed both the Canine Psychology course from The Canine Behaviour Centre and the Animal Care College's 'Understanding the Canine/Human Interface' course. This still didn't completely satisfy my thirst for knowledge so I also did C.O.A.P.E's 'Training for the Future' course which would mean I was qualified to run puppy socialisation classes and I attended numerous seminars and public talks about dog behaviour to try to satiate my newly developed appetite for knowledge.

Probably the most unusual, yet highly informative course I attended was run by Dr Ian Dunbar, an original 'cool dude' who'd had his own television series some years previously called 'Dogs with Dunbar'. I had been used to receiving copious notes when attending any kind of seminar, yet for Dr Dunbar's classes there was a single sheet of A4 paper which held numerous pointers, written haphazardly around it, in various strange fonts. It was a very unconventional approach to study, yet the content of his course was excellent and I came away thinking that perhaps I was finally ready to face the public and to put my, now not inconsiderable, knowledge to the test.

## Tragedy Strikes

Early one evening Scrum was getting out of the bath and I was walking from the bedroom to take Diesel downstairs at the end of one of his periods in 'Coventry', but as the dog tried to stand up he let out an almighty cry. He sat back down again and continued to almost scream in what must have been excruciating pain. Scrum gave me a knowing look as he opened his mouth to speak and, although I knew what was coming, I almost begged him not to say it.

Diesel had just confirmed my most deeply hidden fear - that the hip dysplasia we always suspected he had been born with was far more serious that I ever wanted to believe. Scrum had suspected this for some time and I had always known deep down that this dog was never going to last me a dozen or so years, but I'd always assumed I would have him in my life until he was at least five. At this moment in time he was only two years old.

I had noticed for the last two mornings that the first thing Diesel had wanted to do, on getting out of the house, was to eat huge mouthfuls of grass and make himself sick. I knew that this wasn't a good sign, but had hoped it was nothing serious and had decided to keep an eye on him to see if it continued. I now felt that perhaps this had been his way of coping with the pain he was experiencing upon rising when his hips may have been at their most uncomfortable. So, whilst trying to maintain an open mind and a lightness of heart, I booked him in for an x-ray at the vets for later that week.

Thanks to the advice of Deborah Bragg and my steadily increasing knowledge, we had now managed to make Diesel a far less oppressive force in the lives of the humans in his 'pack'. Yet his hatred of Barney (and more recently Jasper) continued unabated. We had managed to keep him away from the little staffie with no real problems but there were a number of times when he had gone into the garden and decided to throw himself at the pen that contained the highly charged and testosterone fuelled Jasper. This was a recipe for disaster and on one occasion Jasper had taken hold of Diesel's face through one of the 2" x 2" holes in the (thankfully strong) mesh and managed to almost pull off a chunk off his muzzle.

In the early days each of these two dogs had simply ignored its neighbour, but as time moved on they had matured into competitive adults and were now seeing each other as a considerable enemy force to be eliminated. Poppy, however, still loved them both to bits and there was never any question that we couldn't have allowed her to play with one or the other with no concern for her safety as they each loved her in return with equal measure.

One day, whilst still working as an Account Executive for The Health Scheme, I was preparing my notes etc in readiness for an appointment early in the afternoon. The sun was shining and I had decided to open the door to Jasper's pen so that he could lie in a particularly favoured spot where the sun's rays could reach, but there was still a steady, cooling breeze. An hour or so after letting him out, I changed into my suit and heels just prior to leaving to see my client and then remembered that I needed to get something from my car before I could pack my brief case.

In a move that I will both remember and regret to the end of my days, completely forgetting that the door to Jasper's pen was open, I made the fateful error of putting Diesel out into the garden so that he could empty himself, before having to be left alone and I went out of the front door to retrieve the documents from the car.

When I returned, only minutes later, I couldn't comprehend what I saw before me. The gas fire in the lounge was now wrenched from the wall of the fireplace and both Jessie and Poppy were standing almost statue like and watching the events unfold before them. Diesel and Jasper were performing what looked like some kind of tribal dance around one another in the middle of the floor and at first it looked as though they were playing innocently. *Again, my brain refused to work properly at first and I literally laughed out loud, whilst saying, "What are YOU doing in here? Who's this then? Is it Diesel?"*

And then the fog lifted *and I suddenly understood that **THIS WAS NO DANCE.***

Jasper and Diesel were each taking turns to grab at the flesh of the other. Focusing heavily around the neck area, they repeatedly lunged at one another and tried to sink their teeth into the soft skin in an attempt, I can only imagine, to each pierce the throat of the other. At that point I realised that I had to get Poppy and Jessie out of the equation as there was always the possibility that this could escalate even further beyond my control if either of them were to be dragged into the fight.

Mustering all the strength I could, I pushed the battling pair through the door into the kitchen and with one last heave, out of the back door and into the garden. *Looking back, I guess I should have been concerned for my safety as it was always a possibility that, despite neither of them ever having shown any signs of aggression towards me, they could have perceived me as an additional adversary to be dealt with. However, as mentioned previously, it's almost impossible to think straight in this type of situation and I'm sure that adrenaline played a huge part in my actions.*

Poppy, however, had other ideas about being left in relative safety for these were her 'boys' and she was having none of it. She followed me into the garden and stood firmly at the side of the two snarling beasts, yapping repeatedly in a high pitched, still puppy-like bark. It was almost as though she were telling them to stop being so silly and to put their differences to one side.

Fearing even more for her safety, I tried to pull her away but she had grown so huge by now and I was feeling particularly weak in the legs by this stage, so moving her with just brute force wasn't an option. Realising that more drastic action was required, I took off my stiletto shoe in desperation and 'thwacked' her right between the eyes with an firm slap of the heel. This did the trick and as she ran into the house I quickly slammed the door.

Now I had to turn to the much more complicated part of my problem - the two battling bulldogs. With each of them weighing only a few kilos less than me, I realised that hand to hand combat with the two of them was not an option. Scrum had said to me previously (at the time that Jasper had taken hold of Diesel through the mesh) that I should use the hose pipe to squirt him in the face as he would almost certainly let go of whatever he was holding so firmly due to his distinct dislike of water. Trying to keep my head together and think logically, I headed over to the outside tap and turned the handle clockwise as far as it would go to ensure there was sufficient water pressure to create a heavy stream.

A great force of water burst forth from the end of the hose and I aimed it expertly at the now bleeding faces behind the two gnashing, foam covered mouths. The response, if there was any at all, was ridiculously minimal and the water did nothing to deter them from continuing this fight. Moving closer I 'fired' for a second time with my pathetic water cannon, but again there was no reaction and they simply fought on, unperturbed. As I went in for another 'shot' the diffuser at the end of the hose fell off due to the unusually high pressure I had exerted on it and this left me standing hopelessly with a trickle of water running meekly from the end of the pipe.

Undeterred, I soldiered on and approached the brawling mass of muscle to try once more with my 'weapon' *which now, instead of being a once impressive machine gun was more like a child's cheap water pistol.* As I turned the hose on Diesel he lunged once more onto Jasper's neck and took a solid hold. I pointed the hose directly into his face, only an inch or so from his thick strong muzzle. Then, in desperation, I actually put the end of the hose between his jaws in some vain attempt to choke him into letting go, due to the flow of water running down his throat. *(Looking back, I'm amazed I didn't DROWN the poor dog, and lose my fingers in the process, but it's weird how one reacts in a crisis.)*

At one point, I began to focus on a strange and unrecognisable sound. I could hear a desperate and terrified squawking voice asking for help and repeatedly saying the name, "Jasper, Jasper!!!" Only after a second's contemplation did I realise that this sound was, in fact, coming from ME. The noise which was emanating from my mouth was a completely alien sound and was obviously drawn from a much darker place where logic and calm don't exist and panic is most definitely the order of the day.

In my mind it was almost like having two voices in verbal conflict with one another. One of them was screaming for help to anyone who may be able to assist me in this terrible situation. *Whilst the other (the voice of reason) was telling me what a stupid assumption I was making.*

As though ANYONE in their right mind would even consider entering the garden, to try and help me separate two hugely capable animals, who could quite feasibly decide to turn their attentions to the good Samaritan in question was a most stupid belief and one which I had to admit was completely ridiculous. Although Jasper was loved by all who met him, Diesel's reputation had spread far and wide throughout the neighbourhood and no way would anyone with any sense have come to my aid in this situation. Time seemed to have been weighed down and forced to pass at a snails pace. I was incredibly aware of each and every passing second in a slow and steady motion.

*I was recently the witness to a terrible accident on the motorway and, positioned at a thankfully safe distance from the unfolding events, it was almost like watching a slow motion movie. Things happened in front of my eyes and the most minute of details remained in my mind for quite some time afterwards. The events on the day of this terrible fight unfolded in a similar fashion.*

My eventual 'Heaven sent' help came in the form of a split second opportunity when Jasper happened to pull backwards into his pen. Perhaps his innate intention was to 'take home the bacon' and drag his prey into his bed for killing and safe-keeping. Diesel was by no means backing down at this point, but Jasper appeared to have a marginal advantage as he didn't seem to be particularly injured, yet his opponent was heavily scarred across his chest with deep welts inflicted by the slightly younger bulldog's claws.

Realising that Jasper was trying to drag Diesel into the pen, I beat him to this advantageous position and, just as the still-connected heads reached the entrance, I grabbed hold of the door and slammed it into the two, now seemingly fused together, muzzles. It shook me to the core to have to hurt my two most beautiful dogs like that, but my options were limited and a kind of animal instinct was now responsible for my actions. Repeatedly (although, before anyone accuses me of animal cruelty, I believe it was only twice more), I crashed the wooden frame into their bleeding faces and finally, whichever animal had been responsible for the last hold, now released his grip and they separated momentarily, giving me a split second to slam the pen door closed and prevent another opportunity for them to latch on to one another.

Elation filled my head for just a second - *before the logical part of my brain, bravely clinging to the wreckage of rational thought, realised that I was trapped inside the pen with a, now furious, Jasper!* Diesel, however, continued his relentless gnashing at the mesh of the door. The dog-run area beside Jasper's kennel was around 10 feet long so I encouraged Diesel to dash to the far end of the mesh by heading in that direction myself. Jasper followed suit and thankfully, the two of them continued to snarl at one another at the opposite end of the pen. This allowed me a moment or two to make the quickest exit of my life and lock the door; trapping Jasper inside and separating Diesel from his nemesis.

Leaving the two bulldogs to continue their attack through the mesh I ran into the house and secured Poppy and Jessie in the lounge, thus leaving the kitchen free to receive Diesel as soon as I could drag him away from the garden. This I did with the aid of new found, almost bestial, strength, brought on by the sheer panic of the moment. Upon entering the kitchen, and therefore his place of solace, Diesel immediately reverted to his usual self and all swells of aggression were calmed instantly. However, I noted with alarm that he was covered in a multitude of scratches and puncture wounds across the whole of his chest, neck and in particular his ears.

With Diesel out of the way I went to check on Jasper who had now retreated to the comfort of his bed to lick his wounds. As I approached his kennel I could hear a low growling sound coming from the entrance and as I moved closer this warning became more intense. Fearing his reaction to my approach, as he was still full of adrenaline, I decided to leave him alone until his nerves (and mine) had settled and he was feeling more relaxed about being touched. *I couldn't recall seeing any particularly bad wounds on Jasper but in reality he had actually sustained quite a deep puncture wound on his chest which would ultimately require some minor surgery and the insertion of a 'drain' to remove the excess fluid which was repeatedly forming in the hole.*

Adrenaline in the body creates the weirdest reaction imaginable. The initial 'high' for want of a better word, forces us to pick an option between 'fight or flight' - i.e. attack or run away. This was what helped Neanderthal man to battle with the beasties and to kill his prey in order to survive and become the dominant species. Nowadays, we humans are highly unlikely to encounter a sabre toothed tiger when walking down the High Street, so our instincts don't experience the highs and lows they once would have. Humans do still find themselves feeling that initial 'rush' when they suddenly realise that they've left the iron on, or that they haven't paid the mortgage, but on the whole these feelings are pretty tame. However, an approach by a knife wielding mugger, for example, could produce a similar adrenaline rush something akin to that experienced by our ancestors when faced with a wild animal.

After the adrenaline inducing situation has passed, the 'rush' becomes the 'shakes' and a feeling in the pit of the stomach prevails, as though David Beckham has kicked a medicine ball into general vicinity of the solar-plexus. I would say that on the day of the fight between my beautiful 'boys' my adrenaline was at the highest level I've ever encountered. It was, without doubt, the scariest and most horrific situation I have ever experienced throughout my now extensive years of dog ownership and one which I hope to never repeat.

As soon as I was able, I rang Scrum to tell him what had happened and also the client that I was supposed to be visiting for work. I then got changed out of my now ruined business suit and attempted to clean up Diesel's wounds. The sore looking furrows on his neck and chest, although only seeming to be superficial, were certainly great in number. His ears appeared to have received the worst of the battering and they were extremely swollen and full of small, yet bloodied, puncture wounds.

Thankfully there were no obviously serious injuries and when I took Jasper to the vet later in the day to tend to the chest wound, it was agreed that Diesel could wait until the morning as it wouldn't be a good idea to have the pair of them caged side by side in the surgery's holding room and he was booked in for his hip x-ray the next day anyway. Instead, I did my best to clean his chest and neck with a mild antiseptic, but there was no way at all he would let me close to his ears.

Once Scrum had realised that I hadn't been harmed during the fight, his concern for me turned to anger at my stupidity. Not only had I place myself and the other dogs in a seriously dangerous position, but it had resulted in surgery for Jasper and extensive flesh wounds on both participants. As a result of this he was refusing to speak to me and I decided that I would sleep downstairs with Diesel and Poppy that night.

By bedtime Diesel was suffering hugely as the force of the fight had put excessive strain on his already dodgy hip joints. In addition, as anyone who has done any form of unanticipated and extreme physical activity will know, he was aching through the use of muscles he wouldn't normally have used. I tried, little and often, to check his ears but each time I got anywhere near them he would growl at me and I knew not to push my luck. I decided that they could be checked the following morning whilst he was under the anaesthetic for his x-ray and chose to leave them alone.

Deep down in my increasingly heavy heart I was beginning to realise that this night could actually turn out to be the last I would have with my angel. I had already told myself that if his hips were as bad as anticipated then I would not have the right to keep him alive when he was in such obvious pain. Add to that the fact that keeping him and Jasper as part of the same household would be nigh on impossible as there was no real way of keeping the two of them from seeing one another due to the lack of any 'neutral' territory and the whole reality of the fact that I may be shortly set to lose the best friend I'd ever had was slowly beginning to sink in. With this in mind, there was no way in the world that I could sleep - nor indeed had any desire to.

I wanted to spend every last second with Diesel and the fact that my latest 'baby, Poppy, was lying only feet away and feeling left out made my night especially tough. However, something strange was going through my head the whole of the time I spent on the lounge floor on the night of the 4th April 2000. There was a song in the charts at the time called Private Emotion, by the Spanish artist Ricky Martin and although I liked the sound, I hadn't really thought that much about it until then. That night, the words kept running through my mind continually and try as I might, I just couldn't switch it off. The lyrics seemed to almost mirror my feelings for this magnificent animal and they would come to mean a great deal more over time.

For the whole of the night I lie close to Diesel and told him just what a special dog he was. I reminded him of how much he was beginning to change my life as it was solely due to his behaviour that I was now learning to understand the fascinating mind of dogs and the reasons why they do the things they do. I held him, stroked his beautiful honey fur and nuzzled deep into the back of his thick, strong neck whilst letting forth the torrent of tears which were now drowning my heavy heart.

When the morning came I tried to act as though this was just another day but it was almost impossible to hold back the tears as I prepared myself for our trip to the vets. I kept telling myself that they might discover that Diesel's hips were actually fine but that he'd simply strained something and needed to rest. The problem of how we would keep him separate from Jasper was something I would consider once I'd heard what was really going to be good news from the vets and I knew that Diesel was, in fact, in excellent health. *At least, that's what I was hoping.*

When I arrived at the surgery I was hugely relieved to discover that the vet on duty was Heike, a lovely German lady for whom I have enormous respect and who is excellent at her chosen profession. I knew that however hard this was going to be, it was also to be made considerably easier by the fact that I could be completely myself around Heike and didn't have to put on a brave face. As I entered the surgery I could contain myself no longer and I dissolved into a wobbling mess of tears and gibberish. I explained about the fight and the fact that Jasper was already at the surgery and that Diesel needed the x-ray but that he was also suffering as a result of his additional injuries.

Then I faced the hardest statement I'd ever needed to make. I explained to Heike that if Diesel's hips were really as bad as we suspected, then I would want to relieve him of the pain he must be feeling and let her put him to sleep. However, and this was the most important part to me, I would want to do this whilst he was still under the effects of the anaesthetic so that he didn't see me saying my last 'Goodbyes' and he would never actually know that I had been upset. Also, I knew he wouldn't take too kindly to having needles put into his fore-leg and so carrying out this procedure, should it be necessary, would be far easier with him already asleep.

Heike gave Diesel an injection which would make him drowsy enough for her to get him into theatre so that she could then anaesthetise him fully and carry out the x-ray. He already had on his muzzle as no trip to the vets could take place without it, so we headed off to the waiting room to literally do just that, and prepare for the effects of the sedative to begin to work. Despite doing his utmost to fight the drug, eventually Diesel's head began to nod and his legs slowly weakened. I was painfully aware that this may be the last time my darling dog would ever hear my voice and I told him over and over that everything would be fine and that I loved him more than anything in my life.

Heike suggested that I wait in my car and she would signal to me when she had the x-ray results. This was possibly the longest ten minutes of my life thus far and I felt like a prisoner on death row waiting for the pastor to arrive. When Heike called me back into the surgery I was amazed at how, momentarily, my demeanour seemed to change, as though some higher power had given me a shot of strength to get me through the 'science bit'.

Heike showed me an x-ray of a dog with normal and healthy hips and then she showed me Diesel's. The difference was incredible and I could now see why he had been in so much pain. Basically, where there were sharp clear edges to the images of bone on the healthy animal, on Diesel's pictures there was nothing sharp at all. The outlines of his bones were blurred and hazy which showed that the area around his hips was crumbling and would be hugely painful when moving.

I asked Heike how long she felt he could go on if we were to dose him up with the best painkillers available. I was aware that humans can wait for months for a hip replacement and that there must be some kind of pain relief that can be taken in the interim period, so perhaps something similar was available for dogs. That said, I knew that a complete hip replacement wasn't a possibility as this would run into thousands of pounds and Diesel wasn't insured. Her answer was to make up my mind for me as she estimated that the longest he could be expected to continue to walk on these hips, however strong his pain relief drugs may be, was around two weeks.

So there it was.  The news I had been dreading and the answer to my dilemma.  There was no real option other than to allow Diesel to exit this realm of life with as much dignity as he could maintain and to euthanize him whilst he was still dreaming happily of chasing birds, cats dogs......*and, quite possibly, people.*  Although I began to cry again, I knew in my heart that what I was doing was the right thing to do.  My body felt as though my soul had now departed and was watching the whole sequence of events unfold, in slow motion, from a vantage point on the ceiling and I steeled myself for the next new and dreaded experience.

My legs felt like jelly and my heart was pounding so hard I feared that the vet would be able to hear it.  Even from this distance, as her stethoscope hung limply around her neck, I felt it might just pick up the 'boom boom' in my chest and relay the sound to her nearby ears.  We headed to the x-ray room where Diesel lay, snoozing peacefully on the operating table with the muzzle still shrouding his big strong, drooly mouth.  I asked if I could remove this as I couldn't bear the thought of him entering Heaven whilst still being restrained in this way and as he was in such a deep sleep this was given the okay.

As Heike shaved a space on Diesel's leg where she could insert the drug that would bring his end, I wrapped my arms around his scratched and scabby neck.  I looked at his ears; bashed and battered and covered in a multitude of small, bloodied puncture wounds from his battle the day before.  If nothing else, his encounter with Jasper had made it easier to let him go as he no longer looked like the perfect picture of health that he had seemed less than 24 hours previously.

I kissed my boy's sweet, slobbery lips for the very last time, not caring about the drool that covered them and that now covered my own.  For here before me lay the best thing in my life.  He was the 'special one', who had slipped, uninvited, into my heart however briefly and who had shaken my world to the very core.  His job was now done and he was leaving me once more.  He was an angel who had been sent to me, for what I truly believe, was one sole reason - to teach me that there was so much more to dogs and their behaviour.

As Heike injected the drug into Diesel's vein I watched him slip away and I whispered to him gently to run free in the fields and to please watch over me from Heaven, like the angel he truly was. His body lay still, soft and warm and then his mouth opened widely and he let out one last gasp.

Heike checked his heart and he was gone.

# My 'Private Emotion' Pictures

After Diesel's death I felt completely bereft. He'd been my whole world and I couldn't stop crying about the loss of him, particularly as he'd been so young. As mentioned previously, I'd always suspected he wouldn't live to be an old dog as we'd realised early on that his hips weren't great, but I guess I was in a kind of shock at his early demise.

As a way of trying to come to terms with him no longer being in my life, I wanted to create some kind of montage of photographs, almost like a shrine, to ensure his memory lived on and in some small way he was still visible in my life. In the weeks just prior to his death I'd taken a whole roll of photographs (this was back in the days before digital cameras/camera phones and the pictures had been taken on a basic camera with a film which would need to be professionally developed).

I took the film along to the local photography shop and returned the next day excitedly to see the pictures I'd taken of Diesel with Poppy and of him lounging across my knees etc. When I opened the envelope containing the photographs it took me all the strength I could muster not to just crumble into a sobbing heap on the floor.... *the whole of the film had been blank!*

The developers explained that the film didn't appear to have been loaded into the camera correctly so in essence they had developed a completely new roll of film which hadn't been exposed to ANY light at all. I recalled that this same camera was the one I'd taken to my brothers wedding and we'd had exactly the same scenario with all the photographs I'd taken there being blank too.

I was totally devastated at this result as, for some reason, every other photograph I'd previously had of Diesel appeared to be missing. For days I turned the house upside down searching in vane for the absent pictures which would help to keep my memories of my favourite boy alive. At night, I couldn't sleep with the stress of mentally trawling through cupboards, drawers, folders etc, all to no avail.

In a desperate effort to calm me down, Scrum began to join in the search as he could see how upset I was becoming and lo and behold the photographs turned up in a filing cabinet in his workshop in the garden.  At last I could find some peace and begin to put together a fitting memorial of my darling dog.  Eventually, after much consideration, I carefully arranged a number of photo's which depicted Diesel's life from being a tiny puppy (who we used to joke looked like a lion cub because of his honey coloured fur) to just a few months before he died, looking particularly strong and handsome.

I decided to take the range of pictures to a local stationery supplier, where they had a copying machine which could enlarge and reproduce coloured photographs.  I was filled with trepidation as I handed over my chosen images and requested the various copies, as I was scared that if the assistant had asked me anything about Diesel I wouldn't be able to speak.

Then, as I stood waiting for the reproductions to be completed, I suddenly tuned in to the sound of a radio playing in the background, and the song which filled my ears was, you guessed it, Private Emotion by Ricky Martin!!

The lines of the song seemed almost as though Diesel was speaking to me as Ricky sang, *'And I'll be with you, until your tears run dry…'* That moment filled me with both immense sadness and a kind of calm and understanding that made me again believe that Diesel had been sent into my life to carry out his particular task and ignite my interest in dog behaviour.

Once that spark had become a flame, like a beautiful furry angel, he was to return once more to Heaven as his time here was done and his job was complete.  He would remain with me forever and would watch over me until I could finally stop crying over his loss.  Thankfully, as the song left the charts and I didn't hear it so often, I was able to avoid the daily reminders that he was no longer by my side.  It was almost a whole year later when I found that for a few days running I hadn't shed a tear with him in mind and instead had found myself smiling at the memories.

Then, and only then, like in the words of the song, he could rest in peace *as my tears had, at last, run dry.* If I hear the song now it can still catch me unawares and bring me to tears, but on the whole I now hold only fond memories of my angel dog and feel thankful for how he changed my life.

## The Doggy Dilemmas Begin

Several months after Diesel's death we uprooted and moved to the country. We wanted a place with more land so that Scrum could increase the number of bulldogs we had and it also made sense to move closer to his place of work as I wasn't personally affected by our location, due to the fact that I had my office at home. Plus, while we were based in Hull, I was driving Scrum to work each morning and picking him up at night which was using more than my monthly mileage allowance from my employer and costing a fortune in private fuel.

We moved into a house with a fair amount of land on which we could put kennels and, rather than sell the house in Hull, we rented it to an acquaintance - or so we thought – who was receiving benefits and would arrange for rent payments directly from the benefits agency. However, after several months of receiving no rent we discovered that the man had never actually moved into the property and we found ourselves having to pay for both the house in Hull and the one where we now lived. Then, in a further bolt from the blue, Scrum suffered a back injury and was no longer able to carry on working. With a reduced income and double the outlay for property payments we were beginning to fall down a very big hole.

This was the catalyst I needed to take the gargantuan step of launching myself on the world as a now qualified canine psychologist. After much consideration over the name for my business I settled upon 'Doggy Dilemmas' and visited a printer friend to create some flyers which I planned to send to all of the local vets and to display in nearby pet shops. In addition, I took out an advertisement in the local newspaper, sat back and waited for the phone to ring....

Initially I was hopeless at explaining to owners what would happen and the cost of my services. I never really knew how to broach the subject of money etc, but after several calls I got into a routine where I would find out just enough about the problem to know whether or not I felt I could help with it. I would then explain to the potential client that I would visit them at home for a couple of hours to discuss how the behaviour needed to be handled and to demonstrate any necessary training techniques. Following the appointment I would leave the owner with sufficient written information to support all that had been discussed during my visit and my charge for the whole thing would be £25.

**Yes, that's right, just £25!!!**

Much as we needed all the additional financial help we could get, I didn't want to be another behaviourist who clients couldn't afford to hire, much like the ones I had called when my problems with Diesel first surfaced. I believed - correctly it would appear - that I would get to help more owners by charging them a realistic price and I would save many more dogs from being taken to rescue centres, or worse.

Also, by having a set price which wasn't based on a cost per hour, everyone knew what to expect on the financial front and so there were no worried owners thinking that they may have to halt a the training half way through due to lack of funds. Moreover, if I had done my homework sufficiently with regard to the problems I expected to see, then it shouldn't be necessary to visit anyone more than once, or perhaps twice at most.

My idea on pricing certainly proved to be successful and the phone gradually began to ring on a regular basis. After just a couple of weeks I encountered my first really life-changing case and the feeling of elation at realising just how much I 'knew my stuff' would stay with me forever. The problem was surrounding a dog with severe 'Separation Anxiety' and after many years it still remains one of my most memorable cases.

## Only Fools and Doggies

*"Hello. I picked up your flyer in P&J's pet store and it says you can help with 'destructive behaviour'. Is that right?"*

I replied that it was, indeed, correct.

*"Well, my dog's not just 'destructive', he's actually EATING THE HOUSE!"*

The owner went on to explain that he owned a seven month old, male German Shepherd Dog called Del Boy, and he had managed to wreck the furniture, the doors and the carpets. He would jump up at the work surfaces and steal anything he could reach and was continually urinating around the house.

We agreed to meet the following Saturday morning and the owner warned me in advance that the place didn't smell too pleasant thanks to the soiling problem. *As I hung up the phone, my heart was pounding!*

What if this time, like the crazy dog in question, I had bitten off more than I could chew and I was to be out of my depth? So far I had only dealt with really minor problems like walking nicely on the lead or not barking at passers by. This was a totally different kettle of fish and would require extensive research before my visit to ensure I had all of the correct information to hand.

As Saturday approached I read my notes avidly, along with any other information I could glean from my steadily growing library of dog behaviour and training books. Eventually I began to feel confident in what I needed to discuss with the owners and, remembering the advice of a more experienced behaviourist I had contacted in the past, I reminded myself of the fact that it was extremely likely I would have a vastly greater knowledge of canine thinking than the client did.

When I arrived at the house I was introduced to the manic GSD. However, as I entered the lounge I deliberately ignored the dog and spoke directly to the owners. This was no mean feat as the crazy hound was determined to be seen as he leapt energetically from one piece of furniture to the other. The house was far worse than I had anticipated and almost every piece of wood in the room had been chomped on.

The floor was bare, as the owner admitted that the stench had become too much for them and the carpet had had to go, and strips of wallpaper hung from each wall beneath what remained of a previously fashionable dado rail around the centre of the room. By far the worst damage on view was to the once beautiful three piece suite: Made from the kind of plush, cream leather upholstery that a person can almost lose themselves in, what now remained was a mixture of chewed up wooden frame, jutting springs (which stood proud like the visible rib cage of an emaciated creature) and tatters of the previously wondrous hide.

Yet, to my now trained eye, it was the other things in the room which interested me most, such as the two full bowls of dog food placed on the floor along with a vast array of toys. Chewed up plastic bottles and well used 'tug toys' were strewn around the place, accompanied by a number of munched up shoes and hide dog chews. Throughout the whole of the first hour of my visit the dog continued to jump from a chair onto the sofa, to another chair, whilst panting furiously and never actually sitting still. Eventually, after my continued refusal to acknowledge his behaviour, he finally lay down between the owners and relaxed.

After much discussion, it was obvious to me that the dog was very much in charge of its owners and everything he asked for, he would get. If this included the owner's lunch, then so be it. If he wanted to play, he would take a toy to the owners and they would do as he asked. He slept on their bed and would take himself upstairs to lie there whenever he wished. If he fancied a biscuit he would simply stand by the cupboard where they were kept and bark until he was given what he wanted. *In other words, this animal was living in 'doggy Heaven' - or so it would seem to anyone who doesn't understand how canines think.*

Throughout our conversation, I explained to the owners that poor little (big) Del Boy was unbelievably stressed. The man of the house was completely shocked at this statement and hadn't realised that the continual jumping about and panting wasn't just a sign of 'puppyhood' and instead meant something different altogether. I gave the analogy that the household could be seen as a 'business' and without realising, the couple had promoted their dog to the position of Managing Director. Now this is a wonderful job as it comes with many brilliant perks such as food on tap, play whenever requested and a comfortable bed to sleep in. *However, what the MD's job also entails is being responsible for one's employees and this isn't quite so much fun – especially to an inexperienced youngster like Del Boy who was the canine equivalent of a teenage boy in charge of a multi-national company!*

Part of the Managing Director's role is to keep an eye on his staff, to ensure that they are all okay. Yet the owners (ie, his employees) had to leave him alone each day, albeit it briefly, to go to work. This meant that the MD couldn't do his job properly so he had initially fretted about this and his anxiety had manifested itself in a mammoth chewing session to take his mind off the problem.

Upon returning to the scene of devastation, the owner had become understandably angry and scolded the dog for his bad behaviour. Dogs, however, don't think like children and humans can tell them until blue in the face that something they have done is naughty, but because we're dealing in 'past tense' the dog has absolutely no idea what we're talking about, *or what we are angry about.*

Dogs live very much 'in the moment' and when an owner comes home and shows his anger at the destruction that has been done, the dog only associates the anger with the owner's RETURN. The destruction means nothing to the dog - even if we pick up the chewed pair of brand new Nike trainers and shove them in his face! Instead of teaching him that chewing is bad, this behaviour on the human's part only serves to show the dog that whenever he's left alone, when his owner comes back he's going to be shouted at. In anticipation of this scolding, the dog becomes stressed and anxious so he chews something to help him deal with these feelings. The owner returns, the dog is scolded and thus - a horrendous vicious circle is created!

Add to this that we inadvertently make the dog feel that he is being given the role of Managing Director by allowing him access to a steady stream of food, toys and attention and he will continue to believe that he is responsible for the owners and the panic at being unable to keep them in his sights will prevail. By explaining all of this to Del Boy's owners, and giving them a clear set of rules to adhere to, I believed that I had done all I could to help them.

The consultation had been particularly difficult for me as there had been so much ground to cover, but I felt sure that I had dealt with every aspect of the problem. The thing to do now was to leave them to it, and wait and see how things progressed. Bearing in mind that this was Saturday, I agreed to call them for an update the following Wednesday and I left them alone to begin the 'behavioural therapy'.

By the following Tuesday I couldn't wait any longer and although I reprimanded myself for picking up the phone I simply HAD to know how things were going. I spoke to the lady of the house and she said that since I had left, Del Boy hadn't 'stolen' ANYTHING. She said that he had seemed to be leaving the furniture alone and that both she and her husband were sticking to the plan, word for word. I reminded her that she needed to continue to behave in the way I'd recommended and agreed to call back a week later to check on their progress.

I have always felt a great sense of job satisfaction at all of the various roles I have been employed in, but nothing has ever made me feel so wonderful as the feeling that I had helped another dog owner to overcome such a soul destroying problem (indeed, 'household destroying' in this case). I was grinning from ear to ear as I came off the phone and the feeling of elation remains with me still, whenever I think about that particular client and results we had.

During my follow-up call the next week, the owners couldn't thank me enough as they told how Del Boy was now a model dog and hadn't destroyed a thing since my visit. The methods I had given them had become 'second nature' and he had changed into a calm and relaxed dog. Hearing their report of how things had improved so much made me realise that I could have done so many things differently with my own dogs in the past, had I been armed with such a wealth of information and this filled me with a mixture of happy and sad emotions, but more than anything I felt huge pride.

As part of my business I have regularly carried out consultations following referrals from my local branch of the RSPCA. When they first contacted me I agreed to give them a little background on the type of thing I can do by putting together a number of case studies and I decided that Del Boy's story would be perfect for this.

With more than a little trepidation I decided to bite the bullet and call the owners for another update, more than a year after I had first met them. I was told in no uncertain terms that I had completely changed their lives and they reported how they had now taken on a second dog and had absolutely no problems at all from either Del Boy, or the new recruit. Their once crazy GSD's 'demotion' to the role of Tea Boy, rather than Managing Director had allowed him the luxury of having very little responsibility and he was now an entirely different animal.

The owners said that the £25 they had paid me that day had been the best money they'd ever spent in their lives. *And THAT, with the most enormous thanks to Diesel, made it all worthwhile!!!*

## Out-Dated Methods = A Scary Encounter

Before I begin this story, I must reassure you that not all of the doggy problems I've dealt with have involved German Shepherds, but it just so happens that another of my most memorable cases does. I wouldn't want to tar them all with the same unfortunate brush as they're certainly not the only breed I've been called to see, and aren't even one of the most regular types of 'clients' I encounter.

However, in this particular case, the owner of a one year old, male, GSD called me and said that he was having considerable problems with trying to walk his dog on a lead. He said that the animal was lunging and barking at everyone they encountered, be it people, dogs, children, bicycles and more. I therefore agreed a time when I would visit and I requested that the owner didn't feed the dog in the morning, but that he have some tasty treats on hand for training purposes.

When I arrived at the house, the dog was in the garden and I could see him through the French windows which overlooked the rear of the property. Not only could I see him, but he could also see ME, *and that didn't make him very happy at all!* When he spied me through the glass he began barking and scratching like mad at the doors spraying saliva and foam from his incredibly huge mouth as he did so and looking to me like the lead character in The Hound of the Baskervilles.

I asked the owner how he felt the dog would react if he were to let him in to greet me. "Oh, he'll have you" he said, "He had my mate by the throat the other week!" This, as you can imagine, didn't particularly fill me with confidence and I could feel my knees beginning to go weak. (What on Earth was I doing here???? How had my nice, safe, normal life come to this???) Well, there was nothing else for it but to take a deep breath and give it my best shot.

I asked the owner to bring the dog into the house, but to keep him at the other end of the, thankfully, long lounge. I said for him to be kept on the lead and for the owner to keep him still and to leave it up to me to approach the dog on my own terms. However, I also asked for a particularly large supply of treats - something the dog would sell his soul for, such as cheese or meat.

I was given a huge handful of lean ham *(I must confess that I always hate it when the chosen treat is a piggy based product such as ham or, worse still, hot dog sausages, as I don't eat this type of meat myself – long story, and not one I'll bother you with. However, in this particular instance I'd have handled swine entrails if I'd thought it would do the trick!)* I stood back, well away from the entrance to the lounge and began my silent prayer…

As the owner walked the dog into the room the animal exploded into a rage of barking and thrashing whilst rearing up onto his hind legs and clawing at the air between us. All of my instincts were telling me to keep away, but I knew that the only chance I had of making any progress with this dog was to become his best friend.

I therefore steeled myself, turned sideways on to him (to make myself appear less threatening), and sidled up in his direction, tossing the occasional meaty treat at his feet. As I moved ever closer I began to feel his hot breath blow-drying the sweat on my palms as I slowly inched toward him until, at last, with my blood pressure rising up the length of my body, I could hold out a treat for him to take directly from my hand.

**PLEASE, DO NOT TRY THIS AT HOME!!!!**

I'm not suggesting that ANYONE try this kind of thing. This was my own personal decision and it's not something I would want anyone to try without first understanding the complex range of canine emotions and motives for their behaviour. Whilst, on the whole, dogs will mostly react in a similar fashion to certain stimulants, they are each individuals, and some will behave in a highly unpredictable manner, and I *could* have been seriously injured – but this was MY choice, and I'm seriously stating that NO ONE should follow this example. ***If they do, I won't be held responsible!***

Thankfully, as the dog took the ham from my hand he began to relax and to see that I was actually there as a friend, not foe. I handed him several more pieces and then gently slipped my hand under his chin and stroked his neck. After a very short time he had relaxed considerably and within a few minutes more, as my own pulse began to slow, he was lying on his back at my feet allowing me to rub his tummy. (Phew, was I relieved!)

What I had observed when the owner brought the dog into the room was that, not only was he wearing a metal choke chain (sometimes called 'check chain' but don't you believe it, these things are designed to CHOKE), but he was also on a particularly short lead – only around two feet in length.

Therefore, when the dog saw me, something strange that he was unsure of, his 'fight or flight' mechanism set in – in much the same way as my own had done when he entered the lounge. However, whilst he may have wanted to 'flight' ie, move away from me, due to the shortness of the lead he was forced to choose the only other option available to him, which was to 'fight' me.

In addition to this, it's important to know that dogs learn by association, and his association with me was one of pain, caused by the choke chain. Being an animal, and thinking quite differently to the way we humans do, he didn't understand that the pain he felt was actually being brought on by his own action of pulling, but instead he felt that it was all down to the fact that I'd appeared in the room.

What we needed to do was to change his association with everything he encountered on the walk from being one of pain and fear, to something quite the opposite, using the treats we had. I therefore introduced a 'clicker' (a small plastic training gadget which makes a short, unique, sound) to create an association between the 'click' and the arrival of something tasty. Luckily, after just a few minutes practice we were ready for a walk. I also removed the choke chain and replaced it with a thick leather collar, and the short lead was swapped for a strong 'extending' lead to allow him a little more freedom, whilst still being under the control of the handler – initially myself and then, after instructions, the owner.

We left the house and headed to a nearby park where we were most likely to come across a variety of 'obstacles' such a people and dogs etc. Every few paces I said to the dog, "What's this?" and as he looked at me I would click and hand him a treat. After only a few minutes we came upon a young man walking towards us. I prepared myself to pull the dog back if necessary, but didn't drag him tightly into me as this could have triggered the 'fight' instinct and he would have felt restricted at the loss of his 'flight' option.

Instead, as the man approached I repeatedly said, "What's this?" to the dog and each time I clicked/treated him so that in the back of his mind he was subconsciously beginning to think that 'people = treats' as opposed to 'people = pain/aggro'.

This pattern continued throughout the walk and I'm delighted to say that not once did he let me down and in no time at all, when a dog/person/bike appeared, he was looking to me for the click and the treat!

When we returned to the house, after I'd allowed the owner to also successfully try my methods, I asked him how he felt it had gone and if he'd seen an improvement. "I can't believe it!" he said, "What have you done to my dog? That's not MY dog!!!" It transpired that the owner usually wore trainers to take the dog for a walk and he would regularly 'ski' around the field as he was pulled in every direction whilst struggling to hold his furry friend and prevent a nasty incident. That afternoon, he had wandered around whilst still wearing his SLIPPERS, as he'd forgotten to change as we'd left the house and he'd found the whole thing to be a pleasant and relaxing experience.

This had been another situation where I'd had to correct the exact type of behaviour that Diesel had been displaying in the past. Sadly I never got to completely improve things with him as I hadn't had sufficient confidence in my abilities before he'd died. However, I now feel that I could have corrected his behaviour and would one day have been able to walk him safely, without a muzzle, and greeted other dog walkers with a smile.

## Warring Staffies

As time went on my confidence began to grow and I started to feel more comfortable about dealing with a wide range of problems. When a prospective client called me I would know the type of questions to ask to establish what I felt the problem was and this meant I was more readily prepared for the questions I might face and what paperwork I needed to have on hand to leave with the owner.

As mentioned earlier, I now have a particular fondness for Staffordshire Bull Terriers, but had I been faced with the following problem in my naïve 'old days' then I would have run for the hills as the sight of two male staffies wanting to hurl themselves at one another for a fight to the death was a particularly scary thing and not a situation I'd like to get in the middle of.

The owner called to say that his dogs had lived quite happily side by side for several months, but that they'd suddenly begun to fight with increasing frequency and that it certainly wasn't a fight of the playful kind. I asked if the fights tended to always be started by the same dog and he confirmed that this was the case, but that the other one, once under threat, would understandably retaliate, and the whole situation would get very much out of hand.

When I arrived at the house the owners said that they had been keeping the dogs apart as they didn't know what else to do. The situation was reminiscent of the one I'd faced with Barney and Diesel and I inwardly worried that I wouldn't be able to help, but by now my knowledge of how to deal with the problem was much broader than it had been at the time of my own dogs' fighting so I would definitely give it my best shot.

We discussed the two dogs and their individual personalities and during our chat I also discovered that one of the owners had recently changed their working pattern so they were at home with the dogs much more than previously. It's always helpful to find out any changes in the dynamics of the household such as if anyone has recently moved in or out, or if any of the occupants, human or otherwise, have been ill of late. This type of change can affect the way the dogs view the 'pack' structure and they may begin to feel that their roles have changed, which was partly what was going on here.

In addition, whilst the youngest of the dogs had been a puppy they'd been the best of friends, but now that he was beginning to mature, he had begun to see the older dog as someone he should be challenging and as both dogs were also fully intact (ie, un-neutered) they were on an equal footing both physically and in terms of their ability to reproduce – ideal competition for one another.

In conversation with the owners, we established which of the dogs would be the most likely under-dog if placed in a natural situation, but without the involvement of any humans, and they agreed that they would have this dog castrated so that, in time, the other intact dog would begin to see him as less of a threat to his position. Along with this, it was vital that the owners began to demonstrate to both dogs that THEY, not the canines in the household, were the highest ranking, so that the dogs had less reason to fight as the job they were both trying to take on – the boss – was no longer vacant, so there was little reason to see each other as adversaries.

The owners were also told that they should begin to treat the under-dog slightly differently to the more dominant of the two, by greeting him second, feeding him a fraction later than the other one and putting his lead on second when taking them for walks etc. This would help to maintain the pack hierarchy of the owners at the top and then the more dominant, intact, dog, followed by the neutered under-dog.

In situations like this, I always stress to owners that it's entirely possible that the problem will never be solved, however much they apply the rules and work at sorting out the differences. I feel it's a little bit like humans, and sometimes, try as we might, there can be some people who we simply can't get on with. There may be no particular reason for this that we can put a finger on, but occasionally two people will meet and simply won't like each other. However, I was hopeful that these two would begin to become friends again as they'd got along so well before the fighting began so I left the owners armed with lots of information and wished them luck.

By this time I had stopped calling owners after a few days as I felt confident in my methods and I'd pretty much given them all of the information I could, so further discussion would only have meant me going over old ground. The owners knew they could call me at any time if they needed to be reminded of anything, or if they had any questions. However, our paths were destined to cross once more in a very pleasant encounter.

When I first set up my business I was lucky enough to be featured in a local newspaper and the reporter I met with had put me in touch with the closest branch of the RSPCA in the hope that they would pass on my details to anyone who was considering re-homing a dog due to behavioural problems. It was anticipated that I might be able to help them to overcome any behavioural issues so that they wouldn't then feel the need to give the dog to the RSPCA for re-homing and this, in turn, would help the charity to keep the number of dogs they had to care for under control.

Each year the RSPCA ran a huge fun dog show at which I would occasionally judge several categories such as 'waggiest tail' and 'prettiest eyes' etc, but it would also allow me the opportunity to set up a stall inside their marquee where I could help with simple behavioural problems, or I could arrange appointments to visit people with more serious issues to iron out.

During one of these dog shows I looked up from behind my little stall and saw an extremely proud looking pair of Staffordshire Bull Terriers marching happily towards me, followed by an even prouder pair of owners. After a second or so I was delighted to realise that it was the couple with the warring staffies that I'd seen around a month before. Looking at the way the dogs were interacting, it was obvious to anyone that they were the very best of friends and the owners confirmed that they were, indeed, back to being complete bosom buddies.

Again, here I was, having solved a problem which I had endured myself in the past and one which, had I been armed with the right information, I may have been able to correct for my own dogs. Looking back, if Barney had been neutered when Diesel hit puberty, they may still have remained good pals and it wouldn't have been necessary to keep them apart. Had this been the case, then Diesel wouldn't have had to spend half his days climbing up the stairs and damaging his already imperfect hips, thus shortening his life. It's a situation which fills me with both sadness and pride in equal measure, but I'm thankful that I was able to help this lovely couple and their gorgeous staffie boys.

## Barking Mad

Whilst taking part at the RSPCA show, I met with another owner and dog who I'd actually HEARD well in advance of their arrival at my stall.

From a considerable distance I could hear a repetitive bark which was showing no signs at all of stopping and as it gradually got louder I realised it was heading right towards me. The dog, a kind of basset hound looking thing, but not quite a pedigree, continued to bark right up to reaching me and then continued some more. He was barking at the other dogs, but not in an aggressive, or playful, way. It was almost as though he simply didn't know HOW to react to the sight of them. The lady with him looked at me in desperation and asked, "Do you think you can do anything with THIS?"

One of the best tools in my 'doggy bag of tricks' is a set of Mikki Training Discs (more recently re-branded as 'I'll Learn' but still made under the Mikki name). These are a set of five brass discs on a ring which can be used to 'condition' a dog to understand when a particular action is considered unacceptable. They were invented by the sadly late, yet wonderful, John Fisher who's methods played a huge part in my early development and interest in dog behaviour modification.

I've really no idea how he came up with the method of introducing the discs to dogs, but when they work well they can be a fantastic help in modifying many types of behaviour. However, if anyone reading this is thinking of getting hold of a set of the discs, I can't stress enough that;

*They don't work with ALL dogs*

*and*

*The 'introducing your dog to the discs' part of the accompanying booklet MUST be read and adhered to if they're to have any effect at all*

Every dog will react differently to the discs and I've encountered total fear to complete indifference. I've been virtually laughed at by some dogs who almost appeared to be saying, "Come on then, if that's the best you can do!!" and in the most extreme case I was swiftly bitten on the leg. *In fact, in the words of Forrest Gump, 'you never know what you're gonna get...'*

We took the dog around the back of the marquee and I conditioned him to the discs using some treats I had with me. Thankfully he reacted perfectly and responded well to the sound, understanding that when he heard the 'chink' of the discs, he should stop the thing he was doing – which in this case would be the barking.

We then walked him around to the front of the marquee again where he was faced with a multitude of dogs. Straight away he began to bark and I instantly shook the discs at him, signalling that his behaviour was unacceptable. Incredibly, he closed his mouth and immediately stopped the barking!

The owner looked at me like I was some kind of magician (I must admit, I felt a bit like one at that point) and then asked me if she could buy the discs from me. I explained that they were the only set I had at the time, but agreed she could borrow them for half and hour and come back to let me know how they got on.

Half an hour later she thankfully returned (I would have been pretty devastated if she'd taken the discs and not come back as they were the set I'd bought in an attempt to sort out Diesel and I had a strange sentimentality for them). She had a beaming smile on her face and she said that the dog hadn't barked ONCE since she'd left me.

I was delighted as it again demonstrated to me how quickly some dogs can learn, once they understand what it is we're trying to explain to them. I've seen her at the show several times in later years and the little fella is still behaving himself.

## Reading the Riot Act

I received a call from a lady who sounded to be at least in her early 70's or perhaps older, telling me that her little terrier was running her ragged and she didn't know what to do with him. I asked the usual questions to get a feel of what I thought might be the problem and, as I'd suspected, it was fairly obvious to me that he was acting as though it was his RIGHT to push her around.

Whenever I arrive at a property I can normally tell if I've got the right house by the amount of pandemonium which ensues after I knock on the door, and this time was no exception. As I rang the bell, a tiny little wire haired terrier appeared on the nearby windowsill and began barking furiously and darting on and off again excitedly. I could hear the elderly lady owner trying desperately to get him to be quiet and, after some treat enhanced coaxing he followed her into the dining room where she could leave him safely before letting me into the house.

Once inside I could see that the lady was particularly tiny which was presumably why she'd opted for such a little dog, but being of terrier type, he had a huge personality to make up for his lack in stature. After making my introductions and explaining how the session would pan out, I suggested the lady let the dog into the lounge to join us and asked her to ignore him when he came into the room.

Sadly, my advice went very much unheeded as he flew through the door at breakneck speed, barking at me as loud as he could and carrying out a move I tend to call 'the wall of death'. (This is when dogs run crazily across the back of any sofa, chair or cabinet they can find in a continual circle of the room and refuse to stop as, from experience, they've found that the more they do this, the more electrified the atmosphere becomes as the owner gets increasingly animated.) In typical fashion, the lady began to shout and ball at him, repeatedly saying, "No, no" and calling his name, but he completely ignored her and persevered in his lap of honour around the room.

I asked her to simply sit down and ignore the dog, but she found this way too difficult and couldn't stop herself from getting up to shoo him down from the furniture and reprimanding him again and again. In the end I felt the only option was for ME to remove the dog from the situation so that we could have a quiet, sensible chat about how she needed to behave around him, in order to change his attitude.

After first checking with the owner that I would be safe to touch the dog without receiving a nasty bite, she confirmed that he was 'all mouth but no action' and that he wouldn't hurt a fly. I therefore stood up confidently, caught him by the collar, picked him up and put him under my arm, heading for the kitchen. After making a gap in the entrance to the kitchen just wide enough to fit him through, I gently dropped him into the other room and pulled the door swiftly closed behind him.

However, I hadn't bargained for just how quick he could move and I also hadn't realised that one of the laces on my boot had come undone. As I went to walk away from the kitchen back to the sofa in the lounge, I realised that the dog had a firm hold on the end of my bootlace, thus rendering me unable to move more than a few inches away from the door!

I plan my 'consultations' to be around two hours long and over the years I've managed to get it down to a fine art of knowing at exactly what pace I need to be running through various topics in order to finish at around 120 minutes. Some owners will sit completely silently throughout, like petrified children waiting to be told off by the dog trainer (something which I feel really sad about as I'm always eager to point out to people that the mistakes they may have made have probably also been made by me, and that if there are things to put right, it's far better than if they've already been doing everything perfectly and we've got nothing else to work with). Others ask a million questions about some of the strangest topics and I can leave their house with a pounding head and feeling like I've endured a heavy round of 'Mastermind'.

This particular owner, I felt, was going to fall into the category of those who don't really listen to anything you say, but who will simply talk over you and repeat what they've already tried – which failed – and what old Mr Johnson's next door neighbour's cat suggested they should try (which again failed!) Therefore, as I felt the need to get things moving along, I decided to remain where I stood, with my bootlace under the kitchen door, attached to a crazy little terrier who'd caught his prey and had no intention of letting go.

Throughout the next 15 minutes we talked through the dog's daily routine whilst all the time my left leg was banging against the door as I attempted to pull my foot away, and the dog attempted to pull me through the one inch gap near the floor. I must have looked like I was doing some deranged version of the Hokey Cokey as my leg went 'in, out, and shook all about', but eventually he got tired of the game and let me go, so I could return to the sofa and try to continue in a more dignified manner.

At the end of the session, the lady appeared to have generally grasped the things I'd explained to her about why he was behaving the way he was, and what she needed to do to sort him out. I left her with the usual pile of papers to remind her about everything from bite inhibition, barking on command, status adjustment, recall and separation anxiety, and I told her I would give her a call in a few days time, but she could contact me whenever she wanted in the meantime if she had any questions.

Several days later I decided to give her a ring and see how she was getting on. I must admit that I hadn't held out too much hope as I'd suspected she would simply pay my fee, take the information, and then continue in her old ways without much progress. When she answered the phone, the conversation went something like this;

"Hello Mrs...., it's Jo here from Doggy Dilemmas, you know, the dog trainer who came last week. I just wondered how you've been getting on?"

*"Hmm, not very well at all I'm afraid, in fact, he's just the same, naughty as ever."*

"Oh dear. Can you tell me, what are some of the things you've been doing since I came to see you?"

*"Well, after you went, I made a nice cup of tea, let him out of the kitchen and took him through to the lounge for a sit down. I put him on my knee and I read ALL of the information you left with me to him, but do you know what? He's not taken notice of ANYTHING I said!!!"*

I can honestly say that this was not the response I'd anticipated, but it was one which, for once, left me utterly speechless! I always stress to my clients that dogs speak 'canine' and not English (although I've also discovered that they also speak via telepathy – more of that later…)

After a little more discussion the lady said that a male friend of hers was returning from a visit to Australia in the next few days and he'd said that he would be happy to give the dog a home with him and I confessed that I thought that might just be the best option for all concerned.

You meet some strange folk eh?!

## Through the Keyhole

One of the most interesting parts of what I do is, I must confess, the opportunity to take a peek at what goes on in other peoples' homes. I'm not some kind of weirdo peeping Tom, but I do find it fascinating to see how people furnish their houses and the kind of items they keep. I've seen all sorts of unusual décor and visited some highly palatial properties including a couple of wonderful 'halls' which bore the name of the villages where they stood.

At one of these halls, we were trying to discourage a Jack Russell terrier from going through a fence on the boundary of the property so we were walking through a huge meadow which was home to a large flock of sheep. Thankfully the dog didn't bother the live-stock at all, but as we wandered around I spotted something else which I guessed might just have been a significant problem to one sheep in particular.

Through the long, deep grass at the edge of the meadow I could see a young lamb looking around as if it was lost or concerned. As we moved closer I spotted four black hooves waving around in the air and I realised that the lamb's mother was lying on her back and couldn't get up again. Apparently, when this happens, it's essential to get the sheep back on her feet as she will almost certainly die. I don't know the exact details, but I think it can be a combination of the animal choking and some kind of horrifying attack by crows which can finish them off!

Sheep, when fully laden with an unclipped fleece, are particularly hefty and a kind of 'square' shape so the poor thing could never have rolled itself upright. The owner of the dog helped me and, after some heavy lifting, we managed to get the mother sheep back on her legs again and she ambled away with her baby, leaving me feeling both relieved and proud to have been of service.

Although, on the whole, the homes I visit are both welcoming and beautiful, I do recall one house which left me feeling sickened and confused about what I should do next. I'd received a call from a young lady who said that her dog was generally just boisterous and a little excitable and, as she also had a small child, she wanted to make sure she could get him under control. When I arrived at the house, I'd actually written the address down incorrectly but, as luck would have it, the door I knocked at was the home of a relative of the lady who just happened to live next-door. He told me that my client had needed to go out for a few minutes, but she would return very soon, and I could wait at his house if I wished.

As I entered through the front door of the property, I could see right through the house to the rear entrance, which in turn led onto the garden. On the lawn I could see a young child of about three years old and two very large, strong Akita dogs. Now, I must confess that however much I try to tell myself that I'm being stupid, Akitas are the only breed of dog that, for some inexplicable reason, concern me. I've never had any real reason not to trust this breed and I've met some beautiful and placid examples, but I can't help but be worried by them.

These two stunning specimens of supreme canine condition were happily playing around in the garden whilst the young child sprayed them with water from a hosepipe and all looked to be perfectly fine. However, when I asked if they were a breeding pair and the owner told me they were actually brothers (both intact, and around seven months old), I just couldn't wait to get out of there as it appeared to me to be a recipe for disaster with the distinct likelihood that in a month or two's time they would be starting to challenge one another, perhaps with the child in between them. I gave the young man a few pointers as to how he might want to proceed with them and suggested he ask his sister for copies of the information I'd be leaving with her, then I quickly left the house as a shiver ran down my spine.

Next-door, my client had now arrived home and I followed her up the garden back to the house, preparing to greet her 'sweet, but unruly' young staffie. When she opened the door, I was initially shocked to see that her house appeared to have been burgled! However, the state of the place wasn't the result of a break in, and I was shocked to see that this was the way she lived her life. The room was very dark and the smell I encountered almost made me gag as I had to steel myself to remain composed.

As I entered the house fully, I was able to scan the open plan property and on the kitchen surfaces it looked almost as though someone had emptied the contents of her bin in an attempt to find some precious or valuable object which had been erroneously thrown away with the trash. She asked me if I'd like to sit down at the table and I almost refused for fear of sticking to the dirty seat. I chose a chair at the kitchen table, which itself was covered with what appeared to be an old duvet cover, so filthy and stained that I wouldn't have put it in my dog's bed.

Now don't get me wrong, my house is *definitely* not a palace by any means. It's almost impossible to keep a home pristine when it's filled with drooling dogs and their muddy paws, seasonally moulting coats and biscuit crumbs. Plus, working full time and running a business means that when I DO have the time for housework, I most definitely DON'T have the inclination.

But this house was like nothing I'd ever seen before and the worst was yet to come. As mentioned earlier, along with the mess there was an overpowering smell which was like nothing I'd ever known before. After a while, when my eyes had adjusted to the dimness of the room (I'm not sure why it was so dark, but I was almost thankful for that fact as it meant I couldn't see quite what surrounded me), I realised that what was likely to be the source of the smell was a cat litter tray in the corner of the lounge which was literally FULL TO THE BRIM with cat faeces! This tray looked like it hadn't been emptied in months and I would suspect by the smell that the cat which had been using it was an un-neutered male which served to add to the sickly stench which hung so heavily in the air.

As we chatted about the staffie it dawned on me that the young girl not only had the absent cat, and the unruly dog, but she was also mother to a tiny, crawling child, who would likely be approaching said litter tray on a regular basis. My heart was pounding and my mind racing at this possibility and I knew I had to work as quickly as possible to get my information across regarding the dog's behaviour so that I could escape and gather my thoughts.

When I returned to my car I sat quietly for a few minutes and considered my options. My heart was telling me that what I'd seen inside that house was more than worthy of a call to the local social services department as I was sure it wasn't a safe and healthy environment for a young child to be living in. *Added to that had been the potential disaster waiting to happen next-door, but that couldn't really be my concern as I appreciated that my personal feelings surrounding the Akita breed could be clouding my judgement there (again I stress that my feelings for these dogs is unfounded so sincere apologies to any Akita owners/breeders who may be reading this).*

Yet, after much consideration, I ended up listening to my head instead, and taking the cowards' way out by doing nothing. My concern for the child was conflicting with the concern for my own reputation, and safety. If the social services department had gone knocking on the lady's door it would have been pretty obvious to anyone where the tip off had come from and I didn't dare risk the backlash of a some kind of hate campaign or a visit to my home address which, in those days, was on display in some of my advertising.

I still battle with myself on a regular basis about whether or not I did the right thing, as I'm sure I could have simply kept the address and contacted the authorities in several weeks' time, or perhaps I could have tactfully explained to the client the dangers of the cat litter tray combined with a young, crawling child. Either way, it's too late now and I can only hope that nothing nasty ever happened to him.

As was the norm, I called the young lady back after a week to see how things were progressing and was interested to hear that a few days following my visit the dog had run away and hadn't been seen since. I can only imaging that he too had felt he couldn't stand to be amongst such squalor and had headed for pastures new. Inwardly, I wished him the best of luck and I hope he found a new and lovely home.

## Tears and Triumphs

I received a call one day whilst at work from a lovely sounding lady with a Welsh accent who was very distressed about her dog's behaviour. She had a large female shepherd dog which was lunging at everyone on the walk and she'd tried numerous trainers, all to no avail, and so I was being considered the 'last chance saloon'.

I often feel like I ought to be wearing a ten gallon hat and cowboy boots as the 'last chance saloon' label is one which I regularly wear. As a trainer/behaviourist, it's not a great feeling when you know that if your methods don't work the dog could be taking a one way trip to either the rescue centre or the vets, but it's one which I've had to grow accustomed to.

In this particular instance, the poor lady was completely at her wits end and had even contemplated flying the dog out to America to meet with Caesar Milan, the well known 'Dog Whisperer' of TV fame. This would have been a very expensive option, but one which she'd been seriously considering as she knew how much her son loved the dog and she didn't want to let either of them down.

When I arrived at the house, it was obvious that the dog had no intention of working with me whatsoever. I could approach a little way, but I didn't feel comfortable enough to work as closely as I would have wished as she was lunging and gnashing her not unsubstantial teeth in my direction. Thankfully the son was of an age where he was able to simply follow my instructions and we could work on the dog together.

As mentioned previously, the Mikki Training Discs have many uses, and are often very successful as a means of discouraging a dog from lunging at passers by. Luckily, on this occasion, she responded perfectly to the discs and as the son carried out my instructions from behind a conveniently positioned child gate, he began to place treats on the floor and shake the discs where prompted by me until the dog had learnt that the 'chinking' sound meant that her actions were not acceptable and she should back away.

My intention was then to take the dog (and the son, who had control of the lead) for a walk with a huge pouch of tasty treats, and the training discs in hand. In much the same way as we'd trained the German Shepherd who had worn the choke chain earlier on, we used the treats to keep the dog's attention on the son, but when she began to act as though she was about to lunge, he would shake the discs in front of her, forcing her to reconsider her actions and to back away. Once she was then calm, he would treat, and we'd move on.

The discs were merely a way of saying to the dog that the action of lunging was simply 'not acceptable' but that if she remained calm she would receive regular treats. Although they were working brilliantly in this particular instance, I must stress again that they don't work with *every* dog.

Although we could have tried the same method as with the original GSD who had been lunging, this dog hadn't been wearing a choke chain so the motivation behind the behaviour wasn't so obvious. By introducing the discs it meant that, providing they worked as well out of the house as they had done inside, we would be able to demonstrate to the dog immediately when she was exhibiting the 'wrong' type of behaviour and reward her when she was acting correctly.

The effect was almost instant with the dog and with all due credit to the son, he really got the hang of how to use the treats/discs perfectly. Within a few minutes the dog was happily passing complete strangers in the street and upon seeing anyone approach she would look to the handler for a treat, rather than consider lunging at them as she didn't wish to suffer the consequences – ie, a shake of the discs.

The lady owner was so amazed that she began to cry right there in the street as she told me I was the third trainer she'd used and that one lady had been visiting for six months and was yet to make any headway. I was absolutely delighted and I felt confident that the son would be able to carry on with this training and gradually help the dog to accept the approach of passers by.

I explained that the level of assistance I would be able to provide would pretty much stop there as I didn't own a 'stooge dog' (this is a dog who has been so highly socialised with other dogs that it will accept another barking directly in its face and just ignore the situation, thus teaching the other, threatening, dog that the behaviour wasn't appropriate or effective), but for the time being, they had something considerable to work with.

The lady was so pleased that she ended up paying me double and also giving me a bottle of wine as a thank you. I protested that this wasn't at all necessary, but she pointed out that as she'd been on the verge of flying to America with the dog, these few extra pounds were nothing, particularly in light of the swift response we'd seen, so I humbly accepted and thanked her for the opportunity to have helped.

I believe that the above demonstrates how every trainer can have different methods and that it pays to ask around when looking for help with your dogs. Anyone can set themselves up as a dog behaviourist, and in most instances prospective clients don't ask for any proof of expertise or qualifications. Whilst I appreciate that my own qualifications don't extend to a full diploma in *animal* behaviour, focusing instead on only the canine variety, I have certainly studied extensively and been tested on my knowledge. I have also gained a vast amount of experience both with my personal interaction with my own dogs, and with that of many hundreds of 'customers' over the years.

Don't feel cheeky if you need to ask a potential trainer/behaviourist about their background or experience. If he or she is confident in their abilities, they will have no problem sharing this information with you. If you are planning to attend a dog training class, then go along and check it out first to be sure you're happy with the methods on offer and if they suggest you purchase a 'check chain' for the class, then take your dog and leave!

Personally, I actually quite like the way a chain can look on a dog as they glimmer nicely against the fur and can look very attractive, but for training purposes, if your dog is pulling, then opt for a head collar such as a Halti, Gentle Leader, or the crème de la crème, a Dogmatic.

Dogs don't like head collars at first, but if you fit it in the house and then feed, treat or play with the dog, removing it soon afterwards, you can then repeat this exercise until the dog begins to learn - by association - that it's not actually a bad thing as whenever it's fitted he/she receives something good. When you finally venture outside, take LOTS of treats to keep your dogs mind on anything *other* than the head collar and you'll soon both get the hang of it.

## Bichons and Bleach

On the subject of soiling, I've had numerous calls from owners who simply don't know where to start when their dogs continue to toilet in the house. Sometimes it can be a dog which has never been clean from puppyhood, or it can begin to occur suddenly with no obvious reason to the owner as to why it started.

I recall a customer who rang me because she had two male Bichon Frise who had suddenly begun to soil around the house, and in particular in the kitchen, close to the fridge. Obviously this wasn't a great situation due to hygiene issues along with the inconvenience and smell it created, so she was feeling pretty desperate.

We discussed the dogs' daily routine and, as is often the case, I identified areas where the owner could be making the dogs feel as though part of their role was to be responsible for the household. In such situations, part of a dog's 'job description' can include the necessity to mark the territory, ie urinating, to ensure that any passing dog packs will know that this property is taken.

In addition, it transpired that when the dogs had soiled, the owner had used bleach as the primary substance to clean up the mess. To us humans, bleach smells fresh and probably one of the cleanest household products available. Yet to a dog, whose nose smells things in quite a different way, the bleach smells predominantly of *ammonia.* And what does urine smell of…? You guessed it, AMMONIA!

Therefore when we clean up urine using bleach, all we are doing is virtually replacing the scent with the same kind of smell, so the dog simply sniffs that area and thinks, 'Hmm, THIS is where I'm supposed to scent mark is it?' and repeatedly piddles in the same spot. So, in order to fully remove the smell of urine to a dog, the best product we can use is a solution of biological washing powder. That's right, the same substance we'd use to do our laundry, such as Daz, Persil or otherwise. So long as it's 'biological' then it will actually break down the enzymes in the urine and remove the smell, rather than (unsuccessfully) masking it from the nose of the dog.

Another thing which makes dogs more likely to repeatedly soil the property is the reaction of the owner upon finding any mess. If the dog were a child, we could scold it for having done such a thing and show it the offending puddle/pile to explain that the action was wrong. However, dogs think in a *completely* different way to we humans, so doing this type of thing only exacerbates the problem and makes it all the more likely to be repeated.

Remember how I said earlier that dogs live totally 'in the moment', so if something took place a few minutes ago, then it's done and dusted – completely forgotten. Therefore, when we get up in the morning and scold the dog for having piddled on the kitchen floor he doesn't understand that the lecture is for what he did ten minutes ago, but instead associates the telling off with the act of 'reunion'. Thus, when we leave the dog alone again, it will become anxious about the scolding it may receive when the owner returns and this anxiety will cause him/her to soil the floor! And there it is again – *that nasty old vicious circle.*

So, if you happen to find that your dog has soiled inside the house whilst out of your sight (ie, when you're at work/in bed etc) it's VITAL that you don't scold it when you reunite. Instead simply place the dog in the garden whilst you clean up the mess (with a solution of biological wash powder) and then act as though this indiscretion never took place.

Another reason for not scolding the dog after the event is that it will begin to fear the combination of you, him and the urine/faeces. If you tell him off upon finding the mess, he will relate the telling off to whenever this combination occurs, so when he's out on a walk with you he may begin to think, 'Blimey, I'm dying to go to the loo, but if I do it will result in that combination of 'me' 'mum' and 'it', which always means I get told off!' *So instead, he'll hang onto it as long as he can and then when you're out of sight he'll do it behind the kitchen door!*

DON'T decide to leave newspaper down for the dog to soil on unless it's absolutely necessary to save your antique Persian rug. All this will do is encourage the dog to begin to soil on newspaper only, and you'll set up another problem to be overcome. Instead, it's important to reinforce the correct behaviour in the dog by taking him outside regularly with a treat in hand, and when he squats to go to the toilet, issue a chosen command such as 'Wee wee's' etc, hand him the treat, and praise the hell out of him.

By following this routine regularly, the dog will begin to make the connection (again, 'by association') that the act of going to the toilet outside is far more preferable to going to the toilet inside, as if you do it in the garden, not only is it called a 'Wee wees', but it gets you a treat! So why would you then wish to do it anywhere *but* outside??

If you do this often enough, your dog will begin to ask to go outside for the toilet, and will also begin to soil 'on command' due to the repeated use of the chosen name you use for the action. In this way, when you need to leave the house or go to bed, you can make sure he's empty before you have to leave him alone.

Thankfully, the owner of the Bichons completely understood where she had been going wrong, and at the end of this book I'm going to explain how sticking to a set of simple rules can help to prevent these problems from beginning. In her case, the man of the house had recently moved out, thereby leaving the dogs without a 'boss', so they were taking it in turns to fulfil this role until she learnt how to take the reins. It's a similar situation to when Scrum went away with work leaving Diesel to take on the 'top dog' position, but thankfully the Bichon's hadn't begun to fight with either the owner or one another.

## Andie Meets Her Destiny

As I've mentioned, I occasionally would help with queries from people who had spoken to the RSPCA about their dog's behaviour, but in addition to this, the charities local kennels would sometimes ask me to visit to assess a dog's temperament to see whether I actually felt it would be possible for the animal to be re-homed, or if I believed the behaviour to be too difficult to correct.

Thankfully, on the whole, the dogs I met weren't too much of a problem and I would usually be able to give the kennel hands a few pointers as to how they could deal with any simple things such as on-lead training etc. Only once was I forced to make the horrible decision to suggest a particularly aggressive dog should be put to sleep as he couldn't be trusted with a new owner. That dog was a gorgeous young Rottweiler and I hated having to condemn him, but he was simply too much of a liability and had received absolutely no socialisation. Placed in a home with potentially inexperienced owners, particularly one which may have contained children, would have been a recipe for disaster, so the sad decision had to be made.

On another occasion, Sue, who was my contact at the local RSPCA branch, called me to discuss a young border collie they had received. She was one year old and had lived the whole of her young life tied to a table leg in a flat, surrounded by children and an owner who didn't have any interest in her whatsoever. Sue explained that she was extremely timid and that she didn't hold out much hope for her as she was frightened of everything, but I was hopeful that I might be able to bring her out of her shell a little.

When I arrived at the kennels and I entered the pen I could see that the sweet little dog looked like a jester with an almost perfect line down the centre of her face, dividing it into one half black and one half pure white. She was cowering in the corner with her tail tucked completely underneath her and close-by was a puddle of blood stained diarrhoea which she'd obviously passed earlier that morning.

I asked the kennel maid how she was with other dogs and the girl explained that they hadn't been able to take her for a walk as no one could get a lead on her. At the kennels they used soft leather 'slip' leads, which are a one-piece line incorporating a loop at one end which can be slipped over a dog's head and tightened to form a kind of collar. This reduces the need for every dog to wear a collar and means that the girls don't have to put their hands too close to any dogs that may have a tendency to bite them as they try to attach a lead.

In anticipation of what I might be faced with, I'd taken along a pocket-full of little treats so I approached the collie sideways on, and positioned myself beside her, without actually looking in her direction. I put my back against the wall behind her then slowly and gently slid downwards into a crouching position at her side, whilst dropping a couple of treats in front of her nose. Initially she just looked at them and then slowly she took one of the titbits and ate it. I praised her gently and then dropped a couple more.

For a few minutes we remained in this same position, with me dropping an occasional treat and stroking her backside gently whilst offering words of encouragement. After just a short while I was able to stroke her head and allow her to take the treats directly from my hand. Then, a few minutes later I was able to slip the lead confidently over her head and slowly stand up.

I encouraged her to join me in a standing position by using the treats and she did so, but very, very tentatively. Her tail was completely underneath her and the tip was almost touching her chest, whilst her ears were totally flat to her head and she looked petrified. I asked the kennel maid if there happened to be any canine residents nearby who were good with other dogs, and luckily there was a gorgeous lurcher called Daisy.

I walked the collie to the exercise field, with the kennel maid following us accompanied by Daisy. Every few paces I gave the collie a treat and we walked up and down, passing each other gradually closer, until we could eventually gauge how we felt the collie would respond to a full on greeting by the lurcher.

As they slowly got to know one another, the collie's tail was steadily moving outwards and upwards until eventually it was level with her back and wagging gently. She was beginning to relax and had taken to the lead like a duck to water, although this didn't really surprise me seeing as she'd spent her life attached to a lead thus far, albeit one which, in turn, was fastened to a table.

Thankfully, the collie's increasingly confident behaviour meant that I felt comfortable in recommending that she could be re-homed, providing the RSPCA were conscious of the fact that she would need lots of TLC in the meantime to help her to continue to develop her social skills. It was as I was explaining this to the kennel maid that she happened to say the very thing which would change two lives forever, and this was, "It would be perfect if she could go to someone who understands collies and their temperament."

Bingo!! Over my head appeared a huge light-bulb and I began to feel a mixture of excitement and trepidation on behalf of this little female collie. You may recall my friend Andie, who owned Connor, the border collie to whom both Barney and Diesel had taken a dislike? Well, Andie knows collies more than anyone I know. In fact, her whole WORLD is collies. She's surrounded by books, photographs, clothing, calendars, mugs and any other paraphernalia it's possible to find which depicts a collie.

At that particular moment in time Andie had three collie dogs – Connor, who was now getting on a bit in years, but who was still a fit and healthy dog, Kayleigh, who was a female she had rescued several years earlier, and Hanson, another male rescue who had been a bit of a handful at first, but who was now fitting in well. However, up until just a few weeks earlier, she'd also had a gorgeous female collie by the name of Misty. Sadly that sweet girl had suffered from the most terrible arthritis at a very young age and Andie, with the help of her vet, had recently had to face the heart wrenching decision that it would be kindest to let Misty go, and she'd been put to sleep.

I battled with my conscience as I felt that fate was once again taking a hand in my life, along with the lives of several others, and was trying to put these two together. Feeling a little nervous that I was calling Andie whilst her nerves were still raw, I picked up my mobile phone and dialled her number.

"Hello you" she said, "What are you up to?"

"Well, I've got something to ask you, but I really don't want you to feel AT ALL obliged. It's just that I've come across this collie dog...."

I explained how I'd been to visit the kennels and how I'd initially felt there was little hope for the collie, but that she'd blossomed beyond my wildest dreams in a very short space of time. I stressed to Andie that in no way did I want her to think I was suggesting this dog could replace Misty, but that she might want to consider her as she had the perfect environment to help the collie to develop and maybe she'd like to just check her out? After some discussion with her husband Simon, it was agreed that he and Andie would meet me at the kennels the following evening and I called Sue at the RSPCA to arrange the meeting.

As we arrived at the kennels the next day I again stressed to Andie that she needn't feel at all obliged if she wasn't 100% happy with the dog and that I was sure she'd soon find another home as she was such a sweetie. However, I needn't have worried at all as the minute Andie saw her she was smitten. Not only that, but the collie seemed to be very enamoured with Andie too and in one of those special moments an incredible bond was formed. Over the next few weeks, the collie, (whom Andie called Jasmine in honour of a dog I'd recently lost due to health problems), grew hugely in confidence and became an integral part of the crazy collie family.

Jasmine not only became part of the family, but she also began to attend agility classes with Andie who had been taking Connor and Kayleigh, but both of whom had been gradually slowing down due to their advancing years. Jasmine (or Jaz as she tends to be called) excelled at both agility and fly-ball and has literally changed the lives of Andie and Simon. Their house is now covered in rosettes and trophies from all of the competitions they've won and Andie is constantly saying 'thank you' to me for introducing her to Jaz, who she says is her 'destiny'.

In all of this, it's not *me* who should be thanked, but Andie and Simon, for giving that poor little collie a chance and showing her that the world can be a wonderful place. The bond they share is unbelievable and Jaz has become almost as important to Andie as her husband is *(and I can completely relate to THAT particular feeling.)* The two of them are almost super-glued together and Jaz worships her lovely owners and the other dogs who share her life. It just goes to show that there is almost always hope for dogs when people are willing to take things at their pace, and not give up on them without trying to work on their behaviour to help them to adapt to our ways.

## Media Memories

I now regularly receive recommendations from past customers, as well as local vets which is always good for business, but having previously seen how 'Dog Listener' Jan Fennell had appeared on local news features, and in a regular slot on the radio, I decided it was time to try and branch out myself.

I emailed my local BBC radio station to ensure they had my details on file, and I'm delighted to say that they now occasionally invite me onto the station to talk about 'doggy problems' and will use me as a point of reference when such things are in the news. I was also asked to appear (incredibly briefly) on the local BBC news to comment on dog walking etc, so it's all helped to raise awareness of what I do.

I've also made numerous 'appearances' on a local commercial station, KCFM, which has an excellent taste in music, interspersed with interesting articles about local people and events etc.

One of the shows they used to run included a section called, 'After 11' which would have local business people, or anyone of interest, talking about a subject of their choice, so this seemed to be a perfect platform for me to get my details known.

The first time I appeared on the show I was pretty nervous, but thankfully the presenter put me at ease and because there was no actual 'audience' to see, it gradually began to feel like I was just chatting to one person, and not thousands of listeners. Over around a year I made half a dozen or so appearances on the show and would answer a wide range of questions about all manner of problems, from listeners who either called in or sent email queries.

One particular occasion which always makes me smile when I think about it, was when a gentleman emailed in to ask how he should deal with his neighbour who was allowing his dog to soil the pavement directly outside of the listener's house. The presenter laughed as he read out the question and suggested to anyone who was tuned in, that if they were eating at that point, they may wish to wait until we'd moved onto another subject.

It was mid December when I made this particular appearance and when I commented on the question I firstly pointed out the seriousness of leaving dog mess lying around due to the dangers it could carry (in some instances, dog faeces can harbour a dangerous Toxicara worm which, if picked up by humans, can cause blindness). I told the listeners that they should always carry a polythene bag in preparation for the need to clean up, and I then joked, "It's not difficult to pick it up, and it's great at this time of year when it's cold *as you can just put it in your anorak pocket and it helps to keep your hands warm!!*"

The presenter fell about laughing, but quickly realised that it could have been seen as offensive to some people, so he apologised light-heartedly and told listeners that they could now safely resume eating if they were having their 'elevenses'. "Yes" I said, "You can now go back to enjoying your Christmas Log!!"

My Dad had been listening at the time and he texted me to ask 'I wonder where you get THAT sense of humour from??' *Aye, I thought, I think it might just have something to do with you….!*

## My 'Dr Dolittle' Moment

Animal communication is something that I've always found interesting since reading an article many years ago in a daily newspaper.  The piece featured a lady who could 'talk to the animals' and who had dealt with a huge Irish Wolfhound who was unhappy with his name.

The dog in question had been acting particularly depressed and the owners couldn't work out the reason.  The animal communicator consulted with the dog and she told the owners that, for some reason, he wished to be called Egremont.  They began to call him by this weird moniker and his whole mood changed and he became his happy self once more!

Whilst I appreciate that this is a strange story, and one to which many people would simply attribute coincidence as the reason for the change in the dog, it totally intrigued me and I found myself wanting to know more.  Some time later I read a further article featuring a girl called Joanne Hull who had appeared on the TV demonstrating her abilities in animal communication and seemed to have considerable success.  When I checked out Joanne's website I was delighted to learn that she ran workshops in how to become an animal communicator yourself – and this was something I couldn't resist!

I enrolled on a course which took place in Cardiff so it was quite a hike for me coming from East Yorkshire, but I felt it would be worth it if it yielded any success.  I wasn't sure what on earth to expect, but I also couldn't wait to see what would happen.  The course was held in a really old building which completely enhanced the atmosphere and the room we were in was above the kind of shop that sells all kinds of 'spiritual' bric-a-brac such as joss sticks, crystals and Buddhas etc so this also added to the mood.

There were about 12 people on the course, coming from all walks of life, but all very obviously animal lovers. Some were cat people, others were dog trainers and behaviourists and there were several people who loved horses. Joanne introduced herself and explained how she had been able to 'speak' to animals for her whole life and for most of her younger years she thought everyone was able to do the same. She explained that she had gone along to a talk by an American communicator and it had made her realise that this was something she was meant to do, so she'd given up a perfectly safe career to embark on her new way of life, helping animals and people to get along better.

We were shown various slides of animals, some looking mistreated, some looking scared and others who looked downright terrible. Joanne explained that *this* was the reason why it was important for people to understand animals better and to help them to fit into our lives without abuse or cruelty. She then played us some lovely 'mood music' and encouraged us to try to empty our heads of everyday thoughts. She spoke in a gentle voice and told us how to open our minds to receive the information we would get from the animals and to breathe steadily whilst relaxing.

I believe I'm a very spiritual person and I also rely heavily on my instincts, choosing to listen (or not – to my detriment - as is sometimes the case) to my inner voice. I've had numerous experiences of what I consider to be 'psychic' in nature, some much stranger than others, but it's a side of me that I'm always keen to develop and I anticipated I would be able to gain some results, however small, from the knowledge I was getting at the workshop.

The greatest revelation for me was when Joanne explained that we would hear words being spoken in our minds when trying to communicate with the animals she would soon introduce to us, but that we wouldn't hear the 'voice' of the various creatures, and instead it would be our OWN voices we would hear. This completely blew me away because it told me that for years I'd probably been hearing my animals talk to me, but that I'd always thought it was my own sub-conscious voice speaking.

For example, how many times do you suddenly think to yourself, "I'd better just check the dog's water bowl is full" when in fact it was possible that the dog had *told* you it needed a drink and the dish was empty. I mean, why do we suddenly have these random thoughts and isn't it highly conceivable that we're actually picking up on much more of our pets' attempts to communicate than we realise?

After being coached by Joanne on what to expect we were told that a series of animals would be brought into the room and with each one we should ask the same list of questions which would include:

What's your favourite food?

What colour is your bed?

Who is your favourite person?

As previously explained, the responses we would 'hear' would simply pop into our heads and would be spoken in our own voices so we wouldn't, for example, hear a small rodent speak like Mickey Mouse, or a large dog speak with a booming voice. Joanne said to write EVERYTHING down that came into our heads so that nothing would be missed. The questions weren't to be spoken out loud, but would be *thought,* and directed at the animal, in a kind of telepathic nature.

The first animal to enter the room was a gorgeous honey coloured female rat. I appreciate that these are 'Marmite' creatures in that people tend to either love them or hate them, but as my previous fondness for mice suggests, I fall into the first category and I find them really intriguing.

As the owner took the rat from her carrying case, I heard the words 100% clearly in my head, *"She gave me a bath last night – and I didn't like it!"* Hmm, I thought, well let's just write that down…

The rat was then held by the owner in the middle of the room whilst we all proceeded to 'ask' our questions. I wrote down each of my answers, but must admit that I didn't feel I was getting much at all. After a short while, Joanne asked each of us to voice the answers we'd received and then asked the owner the true response. Several people were giving the correct answers…

Food – cornflakes

Bed – red

Person – my 'mummy' of course!

Although it's fair to say, that not everyone got every single question right, I didn't seem to have *any* of these correct, but I tried not to let that concern me as I realised that if I focused on the negative, it might further cloud my abilities.

However, just as the owner of the rat was beginning to pack up her things and place the little lady in her carrying case, she uttered the following words that would completely change my mind about whether or not I could do this;

*"Oh, by the way, I gave her a bath last night and she really didn't like it!"*

I shot up my hand and almost shouted, "Look, look, that's exactly what I wrote the minute the lady walked into the room!!!" Joanne checked my book and agreed that I'd obviously heard the rat correctly *and just to boost my mood yet further, she gave me a sticky gold star!*

The second animal we met was a beautiful big tom cat who acted in a typical feline fashion and almost strutted around the room as if he was some kind of lord and we should consider ourselves privileged to meet with him. I think I may have got one question right, but again I didn't feel any major connection with this magnificent animal.

Then came a lovely little female collie who approached us all with the kind of 'pleased to meet you' exuberance that only dogs can show. Again I 'telepathically' asked the list of questions and although I received some feedback, the most emphatic response I got was in answer to the query of 'who is your favourite person?' to which I heard the clearest 'Tom' imaginable.

When we each gave out our answers I was the only one to have picked up on 'Tom' and was delighted when the lady with the dog confirmed that Tom was, indeed, the collie's favourite person, who she completely loved. I was starting to get the hang of this…!

One of the most interesting things that Joanne explained to us was that it's not only possible to communicate with real, live animals, but that she could also contact animals who had passed on, and even via photographs. This piece of information had been included in the notes I'd received prior to the workshop and we'd each been advised to bring along a photograph of an animal with which we would most like to communicate.

I'd been uncertain which of my dogs I'd most like to 'speak' to so I'd taken a selection of photographs which showed the animals clearly and with a good view of their eyes. I took a picture of Poppy who, at that time, was still alive, a photograph of my mastiff, Mabel, who had recently endured a botched operation for entropion on her eye (and I felt particularly guilty for putting her through it, and wondered if she would tell me I was forgiven), and a photograph of Diesel, who was now, I assumed, chasing around Heaven's fields.

Joanne went around the room looking at each of our pictures and when she came to me she paused for a second to take them all in. After a while she pointed to the picture of Poppy and asked who she was. Joanne then told me that she REALLY wanted to speak to me, so it was this picture that I would use for the experiment.

We were each paired up with another person in the room and told to exchange photographs. I was put with a lady who had earlier on got me quite a bit rattled as she'd insisted on picking on a man who was eating a sandwich containing meat and had accused him of being two faced by on the one hand attending this workshop to help animals, and then continuing to eat them. *Interestingly, Joanne had stepped in to this argument and explained that animals reared for food understand and accept their fate, but that they only ask that we treat them properly whilst they are living.*

The argument had taken up quite a large chunk of the time we had and I was increasingly aware that I would have a five hour drive at the end of the day, so I had hoped to stick to the agenda, but at least the altercation had resulted in that unexpected piece of information.

So, despite my frustration at the wasted time, this lady was to be my partner for the exercise and I had to remain focused and not let my annoyance interfere with my mind. We then had to exchange photographs and to my dismay she handed me a picture of a large chestnut horse. Now, I've nothing at all against horses, in fact I actually find them really impressive animals, but I've never really had any dealings with them and didn't think I'd be able to pick up on much at all. Yet again, however, I was to surprise myself.

Joanne helped us to relax with a few breathing exercises etc, and she again told us to write down every single detail that came into our heads, regardless of how silly it may seem to be. She reiterated that the voice we would hear would be our own, and that we shouldn't allow self doubt to affect what we wrote as every little fact may be relevant.

I stared hard at the photograph of that stunningly beautiful horse and waited for the words to come. What flowed through my mind was a whirlwind of images and facts that I scribbled down as quickly as I could so I didn't forget anything and in no time at all we were being told to calm our minds and come back to the real world. Then it was time to see how we'd done.

The main things which came to me when looking at the horse were:

He loved having his mane plaited

He lived close to water

He loved Christopher

Sometimes he heard a (church) bell ring

He had injured his front, left leg (very specific)

He had a problem with shoes

When I relayed this information to the owner, in front of the class, I was amazed to find that it was all correct with the exception of the 'Christopher' part as the lady then admitted that she no longer owned the horse so she wasn't sure about this particular piece of information. The part that astonished me the most was the detail about his front left leg having been injured – after all, there were FOUR to choose from and I'd got this right!

Next it was her turn to relay the information that she'd received from Poppy. She told me that she got the feeling that Pop was a very *majestic* dog. This was incredible as it's not a word that people use too often, but one of the names I regularly used for Poppy was Majestic Momma after she'd been such a wonderfully serene mother to her puppies. She also said that she liked the new carpet, which initially confused me as Poppy was living outside in a pen with a kennel, but then I recalled that we'd recently placed some carpet in the bed of the dog in the next-door pen, so it seemed that Pop had designs on this and wanted some for herself.

The lady said that she got the feeling that Poppy 'had a thing about poo' which made me laugh out loud. Ever since she'd moved into the pen, Pop had followed this strange routine - whenever she'd gone to the toilet she would let out a mournful wail as if to say, 'get this thing out of here and away from me'. As soon as I'd go out and clean it up, she'd stop. So again, my partner was spot on.

Then she asked me whether Poppy was still alive, or had passed on, to which I said she was still with me. She went on to say that Poppy had said to her, "Thank you for the nine happy years, but it was the tumours that did it." This confused me and I said I'd have to think about that one, but everything else she'd said had been perfect and I thanked her for letting me hear from my very best canine friend.

All in all the day had been wonderful and I felt that it had completely changed my view of how animals communicate and had taught me to have more faith and to trust my inner voice. Sadly, thanks to the earlier argument between the vegetarian and the carnivore, I ended up having to miss the end of the workshop as time was marching on and I knew the day still held an extremely long journey, but I thanked Joanne for being so brilliant and headed home.

Once in the car I called Scrum on my mobile phone to tell him I was on my way. I started to tell him about the day when he interrupted me, saying, "Guess who I saw today?" I asked who it might be and he said he'd seen Barney, our gorgeous, but now sadly departed, staffie! Scrum isn't the type to actually believe in ghosts etc, so this really surprised me, but he confirmed that he'd seen him, lying in the kitchen on an old arm chair we'd place in there for him when he was getting old and used to like to disappear off for his own space.

I queried what time he'd seen Barney, and then the penny dropped…

Barney had been seen at around the same time as Poppy had been saying 'thank you for the nine happy years etc…' – Sadly our little staffie friend had died, aged nine, as a result of cancerous tumours!

*So THAT was why Poppy had been so keen to speak to me – she'd had a message from Barney.*

What an amazing day!

## Saying Goodbye

Much as I like children – particularly when they're around four years old and can begin to hold a conversation – I've never had the 'calling' as I've mentioned previously.  However, one huge advantage that having children has over keeping  dogs is that, if all goes to plan (and I truly hope it does for anyone reading this), they will outlive their parents and it's not necessary for a mother & father to have to consider how, or when the child will die.

When it comes to dogs, this is sadly not the case at all and from the moment I got my first dog, I was acutely aware that he wouldn't last forever and that one day his end would come.  Over the years I've now said goodbye to a variety of beautiful pooches from young puppies who've suddenly fallen seriously ill and had to be put to sleep, to the final hours of my wonderful Poppy and the demise of the once mighty Diesel.

People often say that an owner will know when the time is right to say goodbye to a much loved animal and will sense when the pet has had enough and can no longer cope with the pain of arthritis or another terrible illness. Or perhaps he/she is simply too worn out to want to live another day.

I've faced this situation on a number of occasions and it always leads me to ponder, (in the style of the *Sex and the City's* character Carrie Bradshaw)…

*How do we ever really know when the time is right to say goodbye…?*

When I felt this time had come for my first dog, Scrapper, he had begun to lose all sense of himself and would stand, staring into space appearing to be completely disorientated and unaware of anything that was happening around him.  He had also begun to soil in the house, even right in front of me, as though he had no idea that he was even doing it.

At fourteen years old he'd had a pretty long life and had been reasonable healthy for most of it, but now I wondered if perhaps he'd had enough. On the day I finally decided we should take a one-way trip to the vets, I wanted to do something nice, just for him, and so we headed off to a local wood where he could run free and have a good old sniff around. I then gave him a bag of his favourite doggy chocolate drops and drove to the surgery for a word with the vet.

I decided that I would be guided by whatever the vet felt was the right thing to do as it was possible that, upon seeing Scrapper, he would simply prescribe some wonder drug that would bring back all of his faculties and rejuvenate him again, but I secretly doubted that this would be the case. Having checked Scrapper's heart and his eyes etc, the vet concluded that his liver was failing, and to put him to sleep would be the kindest thing to do.

However, Scrapper didn't exactly agree with him, and what followed was the most harrowing experience I'd had to contend with. Unlike the time that Diesel had been put to sleep whilst already under the anaesthetic, Scrapper was still fully conscious and was determined to fight what was to come. After the vet shaved his leg in order to place the needle into his vein, Scrapper began to run away and was panting heavily in the corner of the surgery, almost as though he knew exactly what the vet was going to do. (And, as per the earlier explanation of how animals communicate – perhaps this was the case.)

Eventually the vet and I managed to hold Scrapper still whilst the poor man did what was necessary, but it had been a difficult and traumatic situation for all of us. The receptionist, who I knew quite well, told me that the vet in question had actually cried when I'd left, so it must have been very difficult for him as he was relatively new to the profession, but he'd still confirmed to me that we had done the right thing.

To this day I still feel that I should have waited a little longer before taking Scrapper to the vets that day, but we were due to move house and I was concerned he would find it all too confusing. Yet dogs are such resilient creatures, perhaps I should have given him the benefit of the doubt. However, sadly I'll now never know, and thankfully another of my dogs would show me just how peaceful an end to life could actually be.

I was at work one morning when Scrum called and said he felt we needed to take Barney to the vets as he was really struggling. He'd been suffering from arthritis for quite some time, but we were controlling it with Rimadyl and he had good days and bad, much like anyone with this terrible condition. In addition, he'd developed a number of lumps on his legs which we knew from experience weren't good news, but we didn't feel he could handle surgery to remove them and as he was getting old, we'd left them alone.

On this particular day, Scrum reported that he was struggling to even get onto his favourite armchair and so I met up with them both during my lunch-break and as we entered the surgery, it never entered my head that I would be saying goodbye to the little fella. The vet checked him over and confirmed that he was certainly in pain due to the arthritis, but that the position of the tumours would also be causing him considerable discomfort. We chatted about the option of surgery, but the vet also believed that due to Barney's age, it wouldn't be fair to put him through it.

After some discussion, it was clear that what both Scrum and the vet were saying was that Barney had pretty much had enough of his time in this realm and was ready to head for ethereal pastures new. Initially Scrum suggested that we should take him home for a final night together, but then we both agreed that such a thing would make it much harder for all concerned and there was a likelihood that we wouldn't be able to face going back the next day, which would only result in further suffering for our little staffie friend.

We agreed that Barney should therefore be afforded the chance to leave us with the dignity he deserved and began to steel ourselves for his sad departure. However, I was amazed and heartened to see that not only did Barney seem to know what was going on, but he was actually quite happy about it! Throughout the whole of the time that the vet was shaving his leg and inserting the deadly needle, Barney looked us both in the eye and wagged his tail happily. It was almost as though he was saying thanks for a lovely life and he'd see us on the other side, but not to be sad as he wasn't upset at all.

This experience really changed my outlook and made me feel that the situation with Scrapper was perhaps due purely to the fact that he was understandably scared of what was about to happen. (Andie later confessed that she'd had a similar experience when she'd arranged for Connor to be put to sleep and that, although it was harrowing at the time, she still knew she'd done the right thing for him.)

Still, it's difficult to really *know* the time is right, but thankfully Poppy made it very clear for me and for that I'm eternally grateful. Scrum had been making the occasional comment that perhaps she'd had enough and was ready to 'go' but I still felt that so long as she happily wandered from her pen for a sniff around the garden whenever I opened her door, then there was still a little zest for life within her and I wasn't going to be responsible for extinguishing that any time soon.

However, I'd watched her over the years becoming increasingly frail and her rear end had begun to fail her from time to time and she would wobble a bit upon standing. One evening I climbed inside her kennel as I'd done each day for years for our usual little chat and some pampering from me to her. She'd always been a somewhat aloof dog and would normally accept my fawning but with a kind of look of disdain as if to suggest that I was lucky to be afforded the opportunity to stroke the Majestic Momma, but this particular time I noticed she seemed to be different.

It was a Wednesday evening and I'd arranged for the rest of the week off work in order to use up some of my annual leave allowance as the end of the company's holiday year approached. When I snuggled up to Poppy as normal, she actually seemed to snuggle me back. She placed her head underneath my chin and nuzzled up to me and into my neck. It was almost as though, for once, she was admitting that despite the aloof persona she actually loved me very much indeed and she wanted to make this clear in no uncertain terms. I never really thought much about it at that point, other than to enjoy the surprisingly close contact and to return the love for her by cuddling her and telling her how beautiful she was.

The following day I got up and went outside to do my usual feeding/cleaning up routine with my dogs who lived in pens and I noticed that Poppy wasn't interested in her food, despite having come out to greet me in the usual manner. Not only that, but as she turned to go back into her kennel, she practically collapsed into it as her legs gave way and she kind of nose-dived into the straw inside.

At that very second, I understood that her time had come and she was demonstrating to me that she'd finally had enough. At eleven years old she was ancient for a mastiff as it's usual for a Neapolitan to only reach around eight or nine and given that throughout her life she'd endured two pregnancies and a rather alarming reaction to some medication for kennel cough, along with her various 'tom boyish' adventures as a youngster, she'd done extremely well to make it to such a grand old age.

I tried hard to fight back the tears as I went inside to tell Scrum of my realisation and to call the vet to book the appointment. Thankfully Andie agreed to meet me at the vets as she knew how much this was killing me inside, and as it turned out, she was a much needed extra pair of hands too. Poppy had to be lifted into the car by Scrum at home, but when we reached the other end of the journey it was Andie and I who had the job of lifting her back out again, and despite having lost muscle mass as she'd aged, she was still quite a hefty lump.

When we got her out of the car she walked a few paces towards the vets and then it was as though her eyes adjusted to what was going on around her and she froze. Living out in the country since she was around a year old, Pop had rarely seen traffic, yet here we were on one of the busiest roadsides in town and she was being asked to walk into a strange building (this was a new branch of the vets which happened to be closer to home than the previous ones she'd attended, but which also meant she didn't recognise her surroundings at all).

Andie ran inside to ask for a nurse to help and two of them came out carrying large towels. We had to place the towels under Poppy and use them like a hoist to carry her into the surgery (talk about an undignified exit!) Once inside she was fine and walked easily into the room where the vet was waiting and I noticed that he had prepared two syringes of the product which would seal her fate.

I lay on the floor beside her and stroked her beautiful saggy face for the last time. Telling her how wonderful she'd always been and reminding her to keep an eye out for Diesel when she got to Heaven, I watched the vet slowly and steadily insert the liquid into her vein. After only half a syringe full she was gone. Soft and warm, she had settled down beside me and breathed her last breath. Thankfully it was a swift goodbye, and this time I knew I'd done the right thing.

After Poppy's death I had a similar feeling to that when Diesel had died and I felt I owed it to her to produce some kind of pictorial shrine. I looked at various photographs, but none of them were really worthy of what I wanted. Then Andie put me in touch with a wonderful local artist who can create perfect pictures using coloured pencils. I'd seen some examples of her work with the portraits she'd done for Andie of her dogs over the years, but I'd never seen anything other than pictures of collies, so we arranged to visit her to examine some of her other pieces, which thankfully were exceptional.

I left a number of photographs of both Poppy and Diesel with the artist and she promised to call me in a few weeks when the picture was done. It was going to cost me £160 which, not being a very material person, felt like a fortune to be spending on something purely for myself, but what the heck, I'd earned the money from my business, so in a way the dogs in the picture had helped to pay for it by being instrumental in helping me to learn about canine behaviour. When the call came that the picture was finished I was really nervous about going to see it as, if it hadn't been quite right, I would have been devastated.

I needn't have worried at all as the picture the artist had created was a perfect representation of the two most important dogs who had shared my life. Poppy and Diesel's heads were side by side and both looking up adoringly. It was exactly what I had hoped for and now hangs in pride of place in my home office and means that I can feel that I've now done justice to my beautiful doggy friends.

## Section Two

## So, how do we gain the perfect pooch...?

## Being the Managing Director of your 'Company'

Having touched on this subject throughout, I'm now going to explain to you how you can make your dog relaxed, happy and less likely to feel he has to be the centre of your Universe and therefore *responsible* for you. *(You may still feel that he IS the centre of your Universe, but the important thing is that we don't let HIM know that!)*

Although I'm acutely aware that some of this information may have been mentioned elsewhere in the book, I'm also realistic enough to understand that some people can't be bothered to read the whole thing, and will want to just skip to the part that deals with their own particular problem. Therefore, apologies for any repetitive information, but if nothing else it might serve as a reminder of what was said earlier on.

At this point I'd like to mention that although I use the word 'his' when referring to your dog's behaviour, I appreciate that you may in fact have a female of the species. It's not that females are perfect – ask any married man and I'm sure he'll tell you that's definitely not the case! – my use of the 'male' reference is purely for ease of writing.

Similar versions of the following information have probably been included in other books on behaviour, as well as being available on the internet. In addition, some aspects of what I say may be considered a little outdated by some, and I'm sure there's a great deal more information which can be added to supplement what's here. However, I know that what I'm saying works well in most cases and has been tried and tested with excellent results many hundreds of times, so I have total confidence in the fact that it is highly likely to help you to improve your relationship with your dog.

You may recall that when dealing with Del Boy, the dog who had eaten his owner's house, I mentioned that I could imagine him feeling like the Managing Director of a huge multi-national company, but that he was a teenage boy and unable to handle the pressure? Well, this is the analogy I often use to help owners to understand the stress they are placing on their dog when promoting him above them in the 'pack' and to help them see how things can be changed.

If a dog is made to feel like he's the boss of your 'company' (ie, household) then he's got a certain job description to fulfil, and a number of perks which go with the job:

A nice posh office with a plush leather chair
*The softest part of the sofa or the spot in front of the fire*

A friendly greeting where you'll smile happily and shake his hand
*A fussy reunion where you make sure he knows you're pleased to see him*

The right to lay claim to the office/factory
*A reason to 'mark his territory'*

A responsibility for his 'staff'
*A need to follow you around the house to check you're okay*

The right to 'look down' on you from his lofty position on the top floor
*A reason to lay above you on the back of the settee or halfway up the stairs*

The right not to be 'man-handled' by his staff
*A reason to snap and tell you off if you try to move/groom/carry him*

The opportunity to 'play' with lots of executive toys such as a nice company car, laptop, smart-phone etc
*Having the chance to play with numerous toys such as balls, tug toys, squeaky toys etc whenever he wishes*

An expectation that staff will hold open the door for him
*A belief that as you approach a doorway, HE should go first*

The best food on tap, and the expectation that you'll give him yours if he wants it
*The opportunity to eat when he wants and to request your food, which you give him when he flashes those big brown eyes*

To expect that when he leads, you will follow
*When you call him, why should HE come to you, after all, he's the leader right?*

To believe that when he calls you to his office, you'll go, without hesitation
*The right to demand your attention, whenever he wishes, by pawing at your leg, or stealing your shoes so you have to chase him*

Are you beginning to get the picture????


In order to demonstrate to a dog that YOU are the boss, the aim isn't to be *bossy,* but to behave with an air of authority that managers command. Again, putting this into human terms, imagine this scene… Whilst walking around a supermarket, occasionally you may encounter a child who is throwing a tantrum and screaming in a heap on the floor. There are two types of approach to this problem that parents seem to adopt:

Pick the child up by his ears, scream in his face and tell him to 'wait till I get you home'
Or

Walk away with an air of 'I really can't be bothered…'

Undoubtedly, for anyone who's seen these in action, I would imagine you'd agree that the *second* approach works best. And THAT is the way to behave with your dog when demonstrating authority. Don't get angry and shout or scream as the dog will simply think that you're incapable of controlling yourself, *therefore you certainly aren't capable of controlling a pack – in which case HE had better do it!*

I believe the two golden rules in dog training and behaviour are:

*Always remember that dogs learn 'by association' therefore if something results in a good association (treat/praise/play), he'll want to do it again.*

*And*

*Reward the good behaviour, but pretty much ignore the bad, so long as no-one is being hurt by you doing so.*

If you keep these in mind you shouldn't go far wrong, but it's also important to always keep thinking about what the dog is actually learning from any given situation and to try to see things from his perspective.

By referring to the 'job description' above, you can start to see why he might follow you around the house – not because he loves you, (although he probably does this too), but because he feels *responsible* for you, and that can be stressful for him. Therefore, because he's stressed, he'll do some pretty weird things such as chew up your house, howl for you to come back and soil the floor in an attempt to protect the property from passers by.


**How Do We 'Demote' Him to Toilet Cleaner?**

Not that I'm saying being a toilet cleaner isn't a worthwhile vocation - it's a hugely important job and I admire anyone who does it for a living, but I don't really believe it carries with it an awful amount of stress. *If the only thing to worry about is how many toilet rolls you have in stock, then I'd guess it's a whole lot easier than having to think about paying everyone's wages, not over-running the marketing budget and keeping up with the competition.*

In order to 'demote' the dog, we need to turn the job description on its head and follow a simple set of rules:

## Control His Food

Where possible, the humans in the 'pack' should eat first, but more importantly they shouldn't leave food permanently available to the dog, instead sticking to two set meal-times each day. If he hasn't eaten his food after, say, 20 minutes, and so long as his head isn't in the dish at that point in time, then pick it up and take it away. If you're a little concerned that he's not eating much, then make his meals a little more interesting by adding some tuna or chicken etc.

Don't give him your food whilst you're still eating it. If he's staring at you (or giving you the 'big brown eye treatment' as I like to call it) and you then give him some of your sandwich/biscuit/steak, then he's going to think that he's obviously far more important than you are, otherwise you wouldn't feel that it was necessary to keep him sustained, and give up your most valuable resource to him. If you really must give him your left-overs, either put them in his dish with his meal, or when he's asking for them, stand up and walk away as if to say, "There's nothing for you." Then call him to you, make him sit (so he has to 'earn' it) and then give him the food.

## Teach Him Some Manners

As you approach a door, try to train him that he should hang back and allow you to go first.  You can do this by using an internal door and tiny treats.  Approach the door with him by your side and as you reach it, show him the treat – put it in front of his nose – and say "Wait".  Drop the treat and whilst he eats it, you go through the door.  Practice several times until he begins to automatically wait at the door for you to go through and then just do this little exercise every now and then to remind him what it's all about.

If he happens to be going upstairs with you, and he runs ahead and turns to wait for you, avoid giving him eye contact as he's higher than you are.   Similarly if he's lying half way up the stairs, don't stand chatting to him, and if he climbs above you onto the back of the sofa, bring him gently down from there.


Limit His Access to Parts of the House

It's not ideal if he's allowed to sleep in your bedroom as this is the 'comfy place' which should be kept out of bounds.  However, I for one know the pleasure that can be derived from waking up snuggling with your dog (see the points about Barney the staffie in the early part of my story) so I'll leave that decision up to you.  What I would say you should *definitely* do though, is keep the bedroom door closed when you're not in there so he can't take himself off to lie in the middle of your nice comfortable bed, whilst you're sitting downstairs watching the TV.


Control His Play

Don't overload him with toys so that he's surrounded by 'his' things and can bring them to you to play whenever he wishes.  It's helpful to allow him access to at least one toy on a permanent basis, as dogs will often feel the need to chew, so ideally he fulfils his natural urge to chomp using a Kong toy or similar, rather than the corner of your dining table, but if he's constantly bringing a ball to you to throw, then HE's dictating what you do, rather than the other way around.  Keep his toys in a cupboard and have regular little play sessions, which end when YOU decide.

If you want to play 'tug' games with him, firstly ensure where possible that YOU can win – ie, you can end up with the toy in your hand at the end of the tug. Do this game at the end of any play sessions and finish by 'winning' the tug toy and putting it, and most of the other toys, away. If you can't win (often the case with big dogs or terriers who will happily hang in there whilst you walk around with them in mid-air) then avoid games of tug and opt for 'fetch' etc instead.

## Remind Him Who's the Boss (in the RIGHT way)

As I said earlier, being the boss doesn't mean you have to be bossy. However, it's worth having a couple of mini training sessions each week, using treats as rewards, just to allow him to see that if you tell him to 'sit' he should do so. He'll enjoy taking part as he's not only receiving some mental stimulation, but he's receiving a prize for doing as he's told, but it will help to reinforce any commands you may use with him such as 'down', 'paw' etc.

## Show Him You Can Look After Yourself

Whenever you reunite with him, don't give him a great big fuss, and instead just ignore him for a little while until he's stopped trying to get your attention. Once he's given up, you can call him to you and have a lovely snuggle etc. *Remember, you're trying to demonstrate to him that he doesn't have to feel responsible for you, so if you don't appear desperate to be back under his wing he'll be more relaxed about being apart from you.*

Whether you're watching the TV, reading the paper, or trying to prepare the dinner, if he's trying to get your attention, just completely ignore him, by looking away and, if necessary, gently brushing him to the side. Don't say anything or give him any eye contact and when he eventually leaves you alone, you can call him to you and give him the attention he wanted. However, don't be surprised if when you call him back he then chooses to ignore you in return, in which case you should go back to ignoring *him*. Over time, this will get better once he understands how his role has changed.

*I remember when I first tried to implement this rule with Diesel and I walked into the room and said to him, "I'm not talking to you – I've got to ignore you" When in fact, I was obviously doing just the opposite!! So, when I say 'ignore' I mean COMPLETELY do just that. It will soon become second nature to you and when you see how much calmer he is it will be worth the effort.*

Once these rules are in place, you should begin to see that the dog is much more relaxed and better behaved overall. That said, you should still work on specific training issues such as recall and details of how to do this will follow later.

I appreciate that I'm asking you to ignore your dog quite a bit to begin with, but please don't think that this means you should never give him any attention – otherwise, why have a dog in the first place? I'm simply pointing out that any attention you do give should be on YOUR terms, and not when he's demanding this from you.

If one of the things he's doing to get your attention is to steal things, then make sure your house is 'dog proof', but leave a few non-dangerous things around that he might still take from under your nose, such as the insides of toilet rolls/small tissues etc, so that when he takes these things you can simply ignore him. Once he sees that the stealing isn't working anymore, he'll learn that it's not worth the effort.

# Dealing with Separation Anxiety

First and foremost it is vital that owners accept that dogs do not understand the concept of "right and wrong" or "spite". Dogs don't destroy things to "spite" their owners for having left them alone. Neither do they understand that whilst it is okay to chew an old slipper, it is not okay to chew on your best leather shoes.

Please accept my apologies if some of this information has been repeated elsewhere in this book, but I can't stress how important it can be.

Dogs are pack animals, so being left alone is alien to them, and goes against their deeply instinctive behaviour. When they chew or bark it is a nervous reaction. They bark to call their pack mates *(their owners)* back to them and chewing could almost be considered the canine form of nail-biting due to stress.

If ever the dog misbehaves when he is left alone it is imperative that you **NEVER EVER PUNISH HIM OR SCREAM & SHOUT AT HIM.** Unless you catch him in the act of being destructive he will not understand what he is being punished for. Many owners insist that their dog looks guilty whenever they return and he has made a mess. The behaviour he is displaying is *appeasement*, ie "Please don't be horrible to me". He simply sees the combination of him, you and the mess and realises that whenever THIS situation occurs he receives some form of punishment – *he doesn't know that it's because HE made the mess that you are angry.*

As a result of this he will relate the punishment to being something that happens upon your return and this will only make him more anxious (and therefore more likely to bark, chew or mess) in anticipation of the stress he will suffer when you come home. In this way, that good old vicious circle will be created and the problem will become worse, rather than better!!! Instead, although frustrating, simply clean up the mess and say nothing at all to the dog.

Analyze your 'leaving routine' to identify the actions which trigger the dog's anxiety by alerting him to the fact that you are about to leave the house. Once you have identified these actions (closing windows/putting on shoes/switching off the television/picking up your car keys etc), you should carry them out more often throughout the time when you are in the home, but pay no attention to the dog whilst doing them – even if he reacts in some way.

In addition, in really extreme cases, you can carry out the following routine to help build up his confidence about being left alone. Where possible, throughout this course of behaviour therapy, you should try to leave him alone as little as is absolutely necessary. I appreciate that this isn't always possible, but if you normally work during the week, it may be helpful to your dog if you can begin the 'confidence building' on a Friday evening, or at the start of a break from work. That way, his confidence will hopefully have increased somewhat before it's necessary for you to leave him for a longer length of time.

By gradually teaching the dog that being left alone isn't the end of the world, ensuring that he understands his place in the 'pack' (see above) and that the owner will return again, he will become more relaxed over a length of time.

# Teaching your dog to be left alone

Plan to leave the room for just a few seconds - perhaps to put the kettle on. For a whole ten minutes before your departure you must completely ignore the dog. *(By this I mean no speaking, touching, apologising, chastising or even looking at the dog.)* When you then leave the room, close the door behind you leaving him alone.

Return again after putting the kettle on, but again, completely ignore the dog.

Whilst the kettle is boiling continue to ignore him and then when it has boiled, again leave the room and close the door behind you so the dog is alone. When you return with your cup of tea, the dog must still be ignored even if he has been crying or is excited to see you. Once the dog has settled down (however long it takes) you can call him to you and give him a love.

By carrying out the above routine, the dog has received no reward whatsoever (eg talking/looking etc) for his behaviour whilst upset or excited, but as soon as he is calm he receives the reward - *in other words, the attention* - he so desires.

Throughout the day when you are at home, regularly carry out the above steps along with your normal leaving procedure, but split it into stages, for example....

Put on your coat and sit down for a while, all the time ignoring the dog.

Pick up your keys/handbag but do not leave the house. Instead continue to go about your normal business - again, ignoring any signs of stress the dog may show and without speaking to him or fussing him.

Remove your coat/put down the keys etc and relax. If the dog is doing anything other than relaxing himself then it is important that you ignore him. However, when he has settled down you should call him to you and give him a fuss etc.

Once the dog begins to accept the above routine without showing signs of stress, you can add to it by actually going out of the door when you have put your coat on etc. However, you should only go out for a minute or so before coming back in again. The dog should be ignored 10 minutes prior to your departure and 5 minutes after returning, to allow him time to settle down when you are back in view. Again, once he has settled you should give him a cuddle etc.

You must practice this action over and over again, gradually increasing the time that you are out of the house. The routine can also be varied by leaving via the back door and returning via the front etc, or by wearing a different coat. *The only thing which **must** remain the same is that the dog is ignored before and after you leave and is only rewarded when he has settled down.*

## Tips to Relieve your Dog's Anxiety When Left Alone

Remember to ignore the dog for at least 10 minutes prior to your departure and don't even speak to him as you leave. If you plan to leave the dog with anything, such as a stuffed Kong toy, simply place it on the floor a few minutes before you go, but don't say anything.

Leave the radio on low when you go out so the house still sounds occupied. However, this must be switched on well before you leave so as not to alert the dog to your imminent departure.

Wear an item of old clothing for a few days (or overnight) whilst not wearing any deodorant so that the material absorbs your own scent really well. When going out, leave the item just outside the door of the room where the dog is left. You can also leave another item of worn clothing with the dog so that he can lay with it if he wants to as a kind of 'comfort blanket'. *(Please be sensible about this – if your dog has a tendency to eat material objects, then obviously don't do this!)*

To help prevent your dog from chewing the furniture and other items you value, teach him to chew things that are appropriate. Use toys that are 'interactive' and therefore require him to use his brain – thereby tiring him out and preventing him from becoming bored. The best toys you can use are a) a well-stuffed Kong and b) a full treat ball. Kong stuffing can become an art form and you will marvel at the concoctions you can create for him to try and remove. Examples are: corned beef, bits of cheese, meat spread, sausage rolls, peanut butter and a filling made of soaked 'complete' food which can be put into the Kong and left in the freezer overnight so it becomes really difficult to remove - and can be given whilst frozen if you wish.

Whenever your dog is given the above toys and he chooses to play with them give him lots of encouragement and praise. To arouse his interest show him a toy whilst saying, "What's this?" excitedly and again rewarding him when be takes it from you. Also, whenever he takes a toy without being prompted he should be rewarded profusely.

Add a few drops of Bach's Rescue Remedy to his drinking water as this can help to alleviate feelings of stress. Alternatively you could give him two 6c capsules of the homeopathic remedy Pulsatilla each day for a week (give it at least one hour away from mealtimes, ideally placing it between his gum and cheek fold so it dissolves there). However, if you would prefer a prescribed drug you can speak to your vet about administering a manufactured treatment called Clomicalm. Please do be aware though that such 'medicines' are not a singular cure and must be accompanied by a course of behavioural therapy as detailed above.

Remember not to make a fuss when you return. You must continue to ignore the dog's advances until he has stopped trying to get your attention – only then can you call him over to you and give him a fuss.

Overall, it is helpful to reduce the amount of contact you have with your dog to allow him to increase his own independence. Don't allow him to follow you around by closing the door when you go to the toilet etc, so he begins to accept that he can't have you in his sight 100% of the time.

This type of problem cannot be cured overnight and will require your complete commitment to the dog, but will be worth the effort in the end.

## Recall – Or Making Your Dog Want to Come to You

When trying to get their dog to return to them many owners become increasingly annoyed and exasperated at the way in which the pet will approach, and then – almost mockingly – will run away as soon as they get anywhere close to the collar.

In many cases the end of a free-running session regularly becomes a game of 'catch me if you can' and is one of the main reasons why lots of dogs are never allowed off the lead during their exercise times.

In order to make your dog *want* to be with you – therefore to return to you when called – you need to become fun to be with. This can be achieved in several ways, using a number of lures (or bribes if you like) including; food, toys, hugs, verbal praise or whatever your dog likes best.

**Things you should NEVER do** if you catch your dog, having chased him around a field for ten minutes are:

**Smack or shake him** – *if, as a child, each time your mother asked you to go to her she then smacked you on the backside you'd soon choose not to go to her when asked, right?!*

**Scream and shout at him** – *When I was a youngster, if I heard either of my parents call for me saying something like, "Here Jo" then I'd happily go to them. If, however, it was a much sterner shout of "Joanne, get yourself here now!" I'd wonder just what I was in trouble for – and certainly wouldn't WANT to go to them. Your dog feels much the same as this.*

## How to Teach Recall

Begin by making sure that for around a week (or longer if necessary) you only take the dog out on the lead and don't allow any free-running so as to avoid any opportunities for things to go wrong.

Begin the training in one room only to begin with and follow this routine:

*Call him to you whilst showing him the treat, but DON'T just call his name, you need to also incorporate a command such as 'Come' or 'Here', eg "Fido Come" etc. Simply calling his name will have him thinking, 'Yes, that's me, but what do you actually WANT me to do?'*

*When he comes to you for the treat, take hold of his collar*

*Give him a morsel of food and some gentle praise*

*Release your hold and let him walk away again*

Once you have your dog coming to you every single time you call him, you can begin to reduce the number of times you actually give the treat when he reaches you. So, you should give a treat the first, second and perhaps the third time he comes but then on number four, no treat is given.

Call him again for the fifth time and again give a treat, and again for six, but not for the seventh time etc. In other words, issue the treats on a very random basis so he's always wondering "Am I going to get something this time? – Oh no. Ah well, maybe *this* time…" and so on.

Only when you are confident that you have this kind of recall 100% guaranteed should you extend the distance you call him from and gradually build up the recall until you can call him from a fair distance. However, each time you do extend the difference, ie if you're in the lounge and you call him in from the kitchen, then initially you should treat him every time, until he's coming without fail, then 'randomly' treat as above.

When you feel you have a good recall in the home, take him out on a long lead (ideally an extending 'Flexi leash' which reaches to about 16ft) and make sure your pockets are full of tasty treats.

Whenever he reaches the extent of the lead, use the recall command and treat him every time he returns. Only when you feel completely comfortable should you remove the lead and let him go further afield. (A beach is a good place to try this as there are usually less places to run and hide). When off the lead, again begin by treating him every time he returns until you're sure he always will and then you can begin to 'randomly' treat.

Treats should change from time to time so he doesn't get bored and not only is he thinking "Am I going to get something?", but he's also wondering "What tasty morsel is it going to be this time?"

In addition, when he is running free and returning to you when called, occasionally put the lead back on when you take hold of the collar, give him the treat, walk for a few yards and then remove the lead again. After a short while, call him to you and put the lead back on, and then a little later take it off again. In this way, he will get used to the fact that the lead going on doesn't always signify the end of the walk. Do this several times during every free running session.

## What to Do If the Recall Fails

**DON'T CHASE HIM** as this will be the best 'game' you could ever play with him. (Obviously, if he's heading for the road etc, then you might HAVE to chase him, but if it's just in the park and he's safe then try the following instead.

To get his attention, make yourself the most interesting thing in the vicinity by running the other way whilst shouting so he thinks "Wow, what's going on over there? I'd better go see…"

As an extreme option, sit, or even lay spread-eagle on the floor (watch what you're laying in) so he can't resist coming over to see what you're up to. Most dogs can't resist sticking their noses in the face of a flat-out owner! When he eventually comes over, *if you can still see him through the steam coming out of your ears,* take hold of his collar, give him a hug and a treat, and only then should you put on his lead.

If he's run off to play with another dog, try to entice his playmate to you with the treats and then you can hopefully get your own pet's attention when he sees the other dog receiving food.

One final pointer – if your dog is a male, with full 'equipment' in place, perhaps you should consider castration. He may be running away to investigate the local ladies and will lose this urge if he isn't being driven by the desire to breed. Castration *rarely* changes a dog for the worse, but in many cases it can *improve* his behaviour by far.

## Teaching Bite Inhibition

Ensuring that a young pup discovers early on that it is not acceptable to place his teeth on human skin is the most vital lesson he will ever learn.

Whilst he is only young a nip or bite or bite administered by your puppy is relatively safe as, although his teeth are needle sharp and can sting, he hasn't developed the powerful jaws that will accompany his adult teeth in months to come.

However, if ever your pup bites you - regardless of whether it hurts or not - it is important that you convey the message that it was *really* painful.  This is done by acting as his young siblings would have done whenever he bit them - in other words you must YELP (CRY OUT) LOUDLY and then TURN AWAY, as if licking your wounds. *Okay, okay, I know this feels silly, but you'll feel a darn sight sillier apologising to anyone who encounters your dog's uninhibited bite when he's an adult!*

As the dog learns not to bite, begin to yelp if he so much as touches your skin with his teeth so his touch becomes increasingly gentle. So long as you carry out this behaviour consistently (and make sure all members of the family do the same) your pup will soon learn that if he bites he loses his playmate, and if given no reward for his behaviour whatsoever.

If you are ever playing with the dog and he places his teeth on your skin you should stop the game immediately and walk away.

The above action should also be carried out if you have an older dog which is biting in any way.  Obviously extra care should be taken as an adult will have a much stronger jaw and can therefore cause greater harm, but the actions to be carried out by the owner are much the same as for a pup.

In some cases, however much you stick to this routine, the dog may persist in 'mouthing' your hands. It's sometimes a breed trait, but it can also be a symptom of the dog feeling that he should control you (so check out how to demote him, above). If this is the case, you can consider using one of the 'anti-chew' spray products available from most good pet stores. Hold the spray behind your back and if the dog begins to mouth you, squirt just a *tiny* bit of this nasty tasting substance into his mouth. After a few goes at this he should soon learn that humans taste FOUL and he won't want to chomp on you again!

In addition to bite inhibition, it is a good idea to teach the dog that when handed a treat he should take it without biting. Show him the treat and as you give him it, say the command "Gently". If he tries to snatch the food you should remove the treat, wait for a second or two and then try again. Continue this, each time repeating the command until the dog does as you ask. Then give plenty of praise as he takes the food in a steady manner.

A dog with good bite inhibition should never receive the death sentence from a judge and could prevent you from being on the receiving end of a massive law suit. He can still be your guardian without becoming a killer and I therefore urge you to carry out the above actions to safeguard his life. Serious but very pertinent stuff eh?!

# House-Training Guidelines

When a puppy (or even an adult dog) enters the human home it has no concept of right and wrong, especially in terms of keeping the house clean. To enable the puppy to learn the rules regarding house-soiling it is important to stick to a regular routine and to be consistent as much as possible.

The following rules should ensure that he becomes house-trained as quickly as possible, and does not develop an anxiety complex:

Take the puppy/adult dog outside regularly - eg every hour, on the hour - and also take a couple of tasty treats. Wait until the *very second* he squats to go to the toilet and then, in a happy voice, say "Wee wees, good boy" or something similar. You don't have to use this command, it can be anything such as 'toilet' or 'empties' etc, but ideally you should use the same single command whether he urinates or defecates, to make it easier for him to understand.

At the same time as saying the "Wee wees" command, you should give him the treat. He may stop 'mid-flow' at that point, in which case you should wait a little longer so he has another chance to continue to toilet and then repeat the command/treat routine.

Each time the puppy wakes up, just after he has eaten, or after a play session, say the word "Outside" and take him to the garden then carry out the above routine.

The old wives' tale of rubbing the dog's nose in his mess when you find it will only ruin your carpet!  In addition it will make the dog anxious when he needs to go to the toilet as he will not associate the 'punishment' with what he has done – especially if he did it hours ago and you have only just come home/got up etc.

By punishing the puppy when you encounter a puddle etc, he will consider a pile of his mess and you being nearby as something to be avoided.  Therefore, he will be unlikely to toilet outside whilst with you and instead will do it out of sight – such as behind a chair.

Unless you have carpeted flooring near his bed, it's not necessary to use newspaper to house-train a dog.  In fact, in many cases, all this will do is teach the dog that it is okay to mess on your latest edition of 'Hello' magazine when you leave it lying around. Instead, regular trips "Outside" using your chosen key word will soon become part of his routine and he should learn quite quickly that it is the place to go as it results in a reward.  The rewards can then be reduced gradually over time as he learns.

By using the same command each time he toilets, he will begin to associate this with the relevant action and you will then be able to encourage him to 'empty upon command' before you need to go out, or at bedtime etc. Remember – keep calm and be consistent and he will soon learn what is expected of him.

Important Note:

When cleaning up any 'accidents' the best thing to use is a solution of biological washing powder as this removes any existing scent better than other cleaning agents and thus prevents the likelihood of the dog re-'marking' the area.  Don't use bleach as this includes ammonia and so does urine, so the dog will continue to re-mark the same spot.

## Dealing With Fearful Behaviour

When a dog feels afraid he will exhibit several different types of behaviour and his body language will become very pronounced and exact.

Often his ears will be pushed backwards at the sides of his head – appearing to be flat.  He may crouch down on all fours making himself appear as small as possible.  His tail will probably be between his legs and very stiff and he may quiver or even, in some cases, wet himself.

The reaction of the owner towards this type of behavioural display is absolutely vital in ensuring that the dog doesn't begin to learn that it is right to be feeling this fear.  For example, if a small puppy hears a hair dryer for the very first time and begins to exhibit the above kinds of body language, an owner can easily make the mistake of speaking softly to the pup and maybe even picking him up and cuddling him.

What then happens in the dogs mind is that he feels that the owner is rewarding him for displaying signs of fear and he may even feel that, as the owner wants to get close to him, then this is showing that there is safety in numbers and that he was correct to be afraid of the 'big bad Hoover'.

Instead of trying to reassure the dog, the best thing is to speak to him in a very matter of fact way as if to say, "Stop being so silly, it's nothing to be scared of." In addition, when the dog exhibits any bravery and begins to approach the 'scary object' he should be rewarded with praise and perhaps even a titbit, so he begins to associate the 'monster' with something pleasurable.

If the dog is afraid of noises, this can begin with something particularly loud, such as fireworks and the problem can escalate into a phobia about any sound, such as a door being slammed, or something being dropped.  Being careful to ignore the initial fearful behaviour when the fireworks are heard is important, but if you have already gone past that stage of fear, it is necessary to begin a programme of 'systematic desensitisation'.

Make a list of the things the dog is afraid of and put the thing he feels is the most scary at the top, working down to the bottom with the least scary thing being last on the list.

Gradually introduce the dog to the least scary thing by occupying him with something else whilst the scary thing is going on around him. For example, if he's a little worried when someone drops a book on the floor, play a game with him and when he's really engrossed, ask someone *in another room* to drop a book. If he pays no attention to it, you can repeat this action several times and then allow the person to come closer and drop the book again. If, instead, he shows fear, simply ignore his concerned reaction and try to involve him in the game again.

Over some time – and this could even take months – move up the list until the most scary things can be around him with no signs of apprehension being shown. To distract him you can either play a game, have a brief training session, or give him a dish of food. In this way he will begin to associate the scary thing with something pleasurable such as eating.

The most important thing to remember is that the above plan must be carried out at the dog's own pace and he should never be rushed from one stage to the next. In addition, it is vital that the owner doesn't revert to showing him too much attention when he shows fear as this will again be interpreted as reward.

To help him to cope with his fear you can also administer Bach's Rescue Remedy or Bach's individual remedy Mimulus (both are available from health food shops or good chemists and a few drops can be place in his food, or you can add a little to his water dish each time it's refreshed).

If the fear is noise related, the homeopathic remedy Phosphorus has been proven to be highly affective. Again, available from the above outlets, you should give him a couple of tablets twice a day, ideally an hour away from mealtimes, and if possible they should be allowed to dissolve between his gum and cheek.

## Barking/Stopping Barking On Command

When a dog's continual barking becomes a nuisance, one way to ease the problem is to actually teach the dog to bark on command. Once this action has been learnt, you can then teach the dog to be quiet when you ask him to.

Many dogs will instinctively bark upon hearing a knock at the door or the doorbell ringing and this can be used to train the dog to bark when asked. Start by arranging for an accomplice to stand at the front door and then tell your dog to "Speak" (or you can use any other command which you may prefer, such as "Talk", "Shout", "Who's that?" etc).

Immediately after you issue the command, your accomplice should knock at the door/ring the bell and the dog will begin to bark. At this point give the dog lots of praise to reward him for barking, but don't use any other treats such as food.

Repeat the above action several times until eventually you can issue the command and the dog will bark without your accomplice having to knock on the door.

Practice this for a few days until the dog is guaranteed to bark when you give the command. Once you have reached this stage, you are ready to teach him to be quiet when you ask him to.

Be prepared with some *really* tasty treats such as pieces of cheese, corned beef or chicken, and tell your dog to "Speak" (or whatever command you have chosen to use).

When he barks give lots and lots of praise so he is really rewarded for the bark, then tell your dog "Quiet" or "Shush" etc and hold a treat in front of his nose for him to sniff (he can't sniff and bark at the same time).

As soon as he goes quiet, give him the treat and praise him gently and in a soft voice so he is encouraged to remain quiet so that he can hear you.

It is also useful during this part of the training to choose a hand signal to be used in conjunction with the "Quiet" such as holding up a finger to your lips or holding your hand flat with the palm facing him etc. This signal should be given at the same time as the command, each time you say that particular word to him.

Go back to the beginning and ask the dog to "Speak". Give him lots of excited praise and then repeat the above step with the treat whilst telling him to "Shush" etc followed by gentle praise whilst he eats the treat.

Repeat this a few times until you can 'turn him on and off' when you wish. If you practice this exercise regularly you should be able to gain greater control over him when he barks at the doorbell etc.

## Walking Nicely On the Lead

One of the most frustrating things for owners is when a dog is pulling hard on the lead and it can mean that they end up avoiding taking their pet for the necessary exercise he requires and then other behavioural problems can develop.

Ideally, puppies should be taught at an early age how best to walk nicely and this is done by using LOTS of tasty little treats. When the puppy is naturally situated at your side you should give lots of continual, gentle praise and regular small treats every few paces.

If the dog pulls to the end of the lead so he can feel it tight from the collar, you should stop, stand completely still and say nothing. Eventually, and it may take some time, the dog will wander back to your side of its own accord. At this point you should treat, praise and move on.

Over time the puppy/dog will come to realise that by walking at your side he's not only getting treats, but he's being told what a good dog he is and, more importantly, he's moving, rather than standing still being bored.

In particularly extreme cases of pulling I would recommend some kind of head collar, but always introduce your dog to this slowly by putting it on him in the house first, ideally at feeding or play times and then removing it again. In this way he'll begin to associate it going on with something nice happening. Once he's got used to that, you can progress to the garden or even indoors with the lead on and use the treats to take his mind off the fact that he's even wearing the head collar. In no time at all you should both get the hang of this.

Please DON'T be tempted to use a choke (or 'check') chain as this can create more problems than it solves – see the story of the lunging German Shepherd earlier on. Also, it could result in considerable damage to your dog and is an outdated form of control.

**Puppy Pointers**

## The Importance of Socialisation

As your puppy continues to grow he will encounter all manner of things throughout his life and the way he is encouraged to react can be the difference between a well balanced dog and a problem pooch.

The 'official' socialisation period acknowledged by canine psychologists is between the ages of three and 12 weeks. However, in reality, socialisation never truly stops (as many owners can testify, seeing the reaction the first time an old dog encounters a hedgehog etc.)

Therefore it is vital that as the owner you fulfill your obligation to ensure that your pup is introduced to many different people, places, objects and animals during his formative months, to prevent everyday things becoming a 'big deal'. *(Please note- I'm not suggesting you take the pup along to a farm to mingle with the livestock - this would be one sure-fire way to lose your dog – but encountering cars, bikes, pushchairs are all helpful.)*

## How to discourage fear during socialisation

As mentioned earlier, if your pup meets something strange and he shows any signs of fear, don't attempt to calm him down by stroking him and speaking in a soothing voice. *(Remember, dogs speak 'canine', not English!)* He doesn't understand that you're saying, "The big bad vacuum cleaner can't really hurt us." What he thinks, instead, is that your soothing tones are saying "That's right puppy, you be afraid of the big bad Hoover, because rather than being nothing to be scared of, it is, in fact, a *very big deal"!!!*

A soft voice and stroking are perceived by dogs to be a form of reward for the behaviour they are currently exhibiting. So, if you don't want him to continue to show fear towards a particular object/person/animal, you must speak in a very matter of fact manner and give him lots of praise and a tasty treat when he then approaches the thing bravely. In this way he begins to see that the object really is no 'big deal' after all.

Once your puppy has had his full vaccinations, you should endeavour to take him to many different places so that he can see that not all people look like his owner and not all dogs are the same shape as him.

If you have the opportunity to take your new pet to a local puppy class this can help his socialisation enormously, but go along and check out the trainer first to ensure you're happy with the methods being used. Modern training should involve 'lure and reward' methods, rather than physical manipulation, such a pushing a dog's backside to the floor.

If you want him to travel happily, now is the ideal time to start taking him out for short trips so that he becomes habituated to the car. Try to ensure he has someone sitting by him, even if he is within a cage. That person can then speak to him occasionally, in a very general way - remember, no soothing tones if he's looking worried - and perhaps encourage him to play with any toys he may have with him. In this way, car journeys become a source of fun as he gets to play and he gets attention from his fellow passengers.

Introducing your puppy to other dogs in your home

Although this isn't always practical, the ideal place to introduce two dogs is somewhere completely neutral to both of them - perhaps at a friend's house where they can meet in the garden. However, if this isn't possible, wherever the dogs are introduced you should follow a few simple steps…

Take the puppy to the 'meeting place' first and allow him to become comfortable with the surroundings.

Remove any toys, bones or blankets which the older dog may be possessive towards.

Allow the older dog to enter and to investigate the puppy. This will include lots of sniffing so try not to be alarmed by this. Talk to the older dog in a happy voice, saying things such as, "Aw, who's this then?" and give him a few small treats so his 'association' with the new arrival is a good one. (In his mind he should be thinking along the lines of, "Okay puppy, you can come again, as you bring cheese!") *However, if the older dog is particularly greedy, be careful not to drop the food as if the pup approaches it this could cause problems.*

If you are concerned that either dog appears worried you can attract their attention and make a fuss of the older dog first when they come to you so he doesn't feel he's being pushed out.

If you feel very nervous about allowing them together at first, the pup can be placed in an indoor crate/cage and the older dog allowed to get used to its presence in that way, until you feel more confident.

When the dogs have settled down you can replace the bedding, but don't allow bones/toys unless you feel absolutely sure neither dog will show possession over them.

In the early days, always fuss your older dog first whenever you reunite with them and ensure that all members of the family know to do this.

At times when you wish to sit with the puppy on your knee it can help to include the older dog by allowing him to sit by your side and feeding him titbits.

Providing you feel comfortable that there is no risk of your older dog actually harming the puppy, you should never reprimand the older dog if it snaps at the pup for biting and jumping on it. Your older dog is better placed to teach the puppy good manners than anyone else, as he speaks the same language, and if it is the pup that is attacking the older dog you should give it a gentle reprimand and praise the older dog when it shows restraint.

By telling the older dog off for snapping at the pup you will raise the status of the youngster and the older dog may come to resent it. This can be a recipe for disaster in the future so considerable care must be taken to get the balance right.

Cage Training

During the times when your puppy is with the family, but you do not wish to play with him, it is helpful if you can place him inside an indoor kennel or cage. The cage should be very comfortable with soft bedding and should be large enough for him to be able to stand up, turn completely in a circle and lay flat out without having to touch the sides.

To introduce him to the cage you should let him play around the room with the cage standing open in the centre. Occasionally throw a toy or treat into the cage and whenever he goes inside give him lots and lots of praise and another treat. In this way he will begin to see the crate as the source of good things. As and when he enters the cage of his own accord, again give him lots of praise and a treat so that he gradually increases the number of times he will want to go inside.

After he has been inside a number of times, close the door for just a few seconds and then open it again. Gradually build up the amount of time the door is closed by repeating this exercise until you can close the door long enough for him to settle down, thus bringing us on to....'King' **Kong!!!**

Kong toys are brilliant (available from good pet shops) and can be bounced, thrown, stuffed and - most importantly of all - chewed! *(You can also obtain different sizes so as your pup grows, so can his Kong.)*

By firstly stuffing the Kong with something really tasty, eg corned beef, hot dog sausages, pieces of cheese, tinned dog food etc you can entice the puppy into wanting to chew on it to reap the yummy rewards. (Obviously you need to allow for this extra food in his daily meals.) When the pup does chew on the Kong you should give him **MASSES OF PRAISE** thereby encouraging him to chew on the toy *and not your home!!!*

Whenever your pup is then placed in his cage for more than a few minutes, he should also be given a very well stuffed Kong. *(Kong stuffing can become an art-form and you'll marvel at the concoctions you can create.)* Then every hour, on the hour, he should be removed and taken to his toilet to do his "Good Boys" etc, given lots of praise for doing so and then placed back in his crate to continue with the chow down.

Alternatively, (and more preferably from his point of view), after coming out of the cage for the toilet he should then receive some play time and lots of cuddles and gentle handling (don't forget to regularly check his teeth, ears, paws and belly so your vet will love you) followed by another chance to 'toilet' before returning to his own 'bedroom'.

Another way of making sure he's happy to enter the cage more readily is to ensure that he receives every meal in there. In this way he will again associate the cage with something nice.

Leaving your Pup alone

As dogs are pack animals, the idea of being left completely alone is hard for them to accept and they need to be taught that this is not a major problem. This can be done by adopting a routine similar to the one detailed in the earlier section about Separation Anxiety.

Whilst you are at home, regularly leave your pup in a room on his own, but before leaving him, don't speak to him or make a fuss (eg, "Don't worry puppy, won't be long" etc) as this will make him think something important is happening. Instead, just leave the room, and close the door.

If the puppy begins to cry, do not return until he stops. This may seem heartless, but if you return whilst he is crying he will learn that he should do this if he wants you to come back. This will effectively teach him to cry when left alone.

Providing he has stopped crying, after a couple of minutes, return to the room. When you do so, don't immediately pick him up or speak to him etc. Instead, go about your business and when he is settled you can give him a fuss and gentle praise. This routine will teach the puppy that being alone is a 'non event' and nothing to get upset about.

It is also useful to leave the puppy with a stuffed Kong, perhaps a couple of other 'activity' toys, such as a treat ball, and maybe even an old item of your clothing which has been worn and carries your scent – the ideal comfort blanket. You can also help him to feel that he has company by leaving a radio on low so he thinks you are still around.

When you return you should remember to ignore him, even if he has made any kind of mess. DO NOT tell him off if he has done anything wrong as you will make his behaviour worse. He will begin to anticipate a telling off each time you leave him and is likely to chew/mess etc even more, to help him cope with the anticipated stress. However, if you follow the above routine and gradually get him used to being left alone he should soon learn to accept it.


Feeding

Feeding times are ultimately up to the owner as it's a good idea to make sure that they fit in with your own routine, but in the pup's early months it is also important to make sure that he gets enough nutrition.

Personally, I believe a puppy should be fed four times a day up to three months of age (two meat meals and two milky meals, eg weetabix/softened cornflakes, using a proper puppy milk powder, rather than cows' milk which can be hard for dogs to digest). From three months he can be fed three times a day if possible and reduced down to twice a day from six months of age.

I would always recommend that you continue to feed your dog twice a day, rather than only once as some owners suggest. Feeding only once a day won't necessarily harm the dog, but I know how bad I feel if I have to miss a meal and I can get pretty irritable, so I wouldn't wish that feeling on my dog!

To ensure your pup learns his position in the 'pack' it's best if you can make his mealtimes after yours so that he is lower down the 'pecking order'. In addition to this, from three months onwards, don't leave permanent food down for the dog. If you put the dish down and he doesn't eat it all, take the dish away after about 20 minutes. In this way he learns that he must eat when it is provided by the 'leader', or else he will miss his chance. If you continue to leave him with a well stuffed Kong, he won't go hungry.

Many owners routinely remove the dish whilst the dog is mid-munch in order to teach him that it is okay for people to approach the dish. Now, if I was in the middle of my Sunday lunch and someone kept taking it away from me (even if they then gave it back) I'd get pretty fed up about it. Eventually I'd probably end up growling at them and would begin to feel quite wary whenever they came near whilst I was eating.

Instead, if they came along and put an extra Yorkshire pudding on my plate, then I would welcome them with open arms! So, to ensure your pup is happy for you to approach the dish when he's in the middle of a meal, every now and then, move in closer and add something really nice to his dish. Maybe even hold the edge of the bowl whilst you're doing it. In this way, he's going to learn that it's fine when you approach because the meal gets even nicer.

Basic Obedience Training

As your puppy begins to mature he may begin to take advantage of the fuss he has been given in the past whilst he was such a cute little bundle of fur. In order to maintain a good level of control over him you should endeavour to carry out daily training sessions – even 5 minutes will do – so that he continues to accept commands from you.

Training should always include the use of treats - and the better the treats, the more likely you'll get a good response. Use small treats instead of great big chews etc so the puppy can eat them easily and quickly.

Teaching a 'Sit' for example is really simple. Hold the treat above the puppy's nose and after a selection of wiggles he should eventually put his backside on the floor (PLEASE BE PATIENT!) The *very second* he does so, give him the treat and say "Sit" in an excited voice and give lots of praise. Repeat this a few times and soon you should find that the puppy automatically sits when he sees you hold a treat up as he has learnt that it is the action of putting his backside on the floor which gets him the treat, and he will begin to associate this act with the 'Sit' command.

To teach the pup to lie down you can get him into a sit position and then hold a treat under his nose this time. Gently lure him down to the floor and – again, after some wiggling – he will *eventually* put his stomach on the floor. The *second* he does so, drop the treat in front of him and say "Down" excitedly followed by lots of praise. Repeat again until the pup is lying down as soon as he sees the treat.

If you want to be extra clever, you can incorporate the use of hand signals when doing the training. For example, whenever you say "Sit" you can show the dog the palm of your hand, hold up one finger, or even scratch your nose! By always demonstrating the hand signal at the same time as giving the command the dog will learn to respond to this too.

## Bringing Home a New Born Baby into the House

In numerous cases, couples who move in together may opt to get a dog as they are not yet ready for children. Inevitably thing can move on and eventually they may wish to add to their family with a 'baby' of the human variety, at which point they are concerned about how to include the dog in this and to facilitate a relaxed introduction.

I would always recommend that before the baby comes along, the owners should be ensuring that the dog understands his position in the 'pack' so that it's not HIS responsibility to decide who is allowed into the house. This can be done as explained earlier in the section about being the Managing Director of your 'Company'.

A few weeks before the newborn comes along, it's worthwhile investing in a 'baby-sized' doll. Both parents can then take turns to carry this around the house so that the dog becomes accustomed to the fact that something else is taking up the owners' attention. In addition, if you are able to record the sound of a baby crying (perhaps on the television – I'm not suggesting you go around prodding kiddies to make them howl!!) If the dog shows an interest in the 'baby' then you should praise him and perhaps even give him the occasional treat.

When the baby is born, assuming this is away from the home (or at least, away from the dog), then the father of the child can take a brand new face cloth or similar and gently wipe the baby to pick up the scent. This can then be shown to the dog so that he can get used to the newborn's smell, before the little one is brought into the house.

The actual introduction is bound to be a little worrying for the parents, but by being patient with the dog and accepting that he is likely to want to sniff the baby things should settle down okay. Obviously, take considerable care not to put the baby too close to the dog to start with, but if he shows interest in the child then give him a few small treats, so he thinks that the baby's arrival is a good thing.

I hope it goes without saying that leaving a child unaccompanied with a dog is a definite 'no no' however well you feel you can trust your pet. Babies smell very interesting – particularly with a full nappy – so you should ALWAYS supervise the situation when your dog/child are together.

## The Last Word

So, that's it. I've said all I wanted to say, I've possibly rambled on, and in parts I know I have repeated myself. However, if the information contained in this book can help just one owner then it's been worth my efforts.

I've thoroughly enjoyed the process of writing this and at times it's been extremely cathartic as I've laid several ghosts to rest and got things off my chest that I wanted to say.

I hope you've enjoyed my story and if all goes well, perhaps I'll write some more. (I've already got an idea for a range of books for children so I think that might be my next big venture.)

The next time you spend any time with a dog, try to put yourself in his shoes and see things a little more as he does. Also, if you can manage to clear your mind and listen to what he's 'saying' you never know what you might hear…!

Best wishes to you and your canine companions.

Many thanks.

Jo Wood.
Doggy Dilemmas
x

Printed in Great Britain
by Amazon.co.uk, Ltd.,
Marston Gate.